The Hungry Home Inspector 2nd Edition:

HUNGRIER.

Why Some Inspectors are Always Hungry for More, While Others Just Go Hungry.

P. Nathan Thornberry

Dan Huber

Paul Zak

Bob Pearson

Mike Crow

Mike Doerr

The Hungry Home Inspector 2nd Edition: HUNGRIER.
Why Some Inspectors are Always Hungry for More,
While Others Are Still Going Hungry.
P. Nathan Thornberry, Dan Huber, Paul Zak, Bob Pearson, Mike
Crow, Mike Doerr

Residential Warranty Services/The Inspector Services Group
698 Pro Med Lane
Carmel, IN 46032
Inspectorservicesgroup.com

ISBN 978-0-692-35324-0

Cover design by Danelle Smart & Tiffani Blackburn
Editing by Jenifer Costner & Petra Ritchie
Bellsouth Tower ©2007 Chris Wage
All other photographs courtesy Freebase.com under license CC-BY

Project Manager: Nathan Ehman

Orders by U.S. trade bookstores and wholesalers. Please contact
RWS: Tel: (800) 544-8156; Fax: (877) 307-7056 or visit
inspectorservicesgroup.com

Printed in the United States of America

First Edition July 2012. Second Edition January 2015.

Table of Contents

This book is dedicated to all of the inspectors who work harder than they have to.

I hope this book helps. The last one did! When you're ready to take it to the next level, check out Change|Up: A Guide to Going Big!

Sincerely,

P. Nathan Thornberry
www.Nathan.tv

Tributes

"The way I look at the home inspection industry is this: there are two types of people in the business; those who provide great home inspections and those who are in the business of providing great home inspections. The difference is critical. This book should help readers determine which they are and how to change it if that is their desire."

Kathleen A. Kuhn, CFE
President, HouseMaster

"Any inspector that reads this book and understands it will double their business. Incredible Read!"

Nick Gromicko
Founder, InterNACHI

"This book is for anyone interested in the home inspection business. Nathan combines a deep understanding of the business with a smart marketer and business operator's point of view to provide valuable information for building a successful home inspection business. In an industry that is undergoing seismic shifts, Thornberry brings a practical and informed perspective to readers. Whether looking to be an independent owner/operator or part of a franchise brand, this book provides a useful understanding of the industry and operating a business in it. Well worth the read."

Dan Steward
President & CEO, Pillar to Post Home Inspectors

"Awesome! This will increase any inspector's business- read it over and over again...if you don't, your competition will! Want to make lots of money and live a happy life as a home inspector? You must read this book!"

Dominic Maricic
President, Home Inspector Pro

"Reading this book has inspired and pushed me and my business to new levels. This is a book you really don't want your competition reading."

Charles Bulfer
Vegas Inspect LLC

"The Information in this book not only has improved my business but it has improved me on a personal level and has become a must read for all the inspectors I have hired."

James Ward
Class Act Inspections, LLC

"This is a MUST read for all home inspectors."

Bob Pearson
Allen Insurance Group

"Well written, great information, and a must read for any home inspector."

Brian Wetzel
HouseMaster

"Great information to take your business to the next level!"

Lee Harless
Safe & Sound Inspection Services, LLC

"Every time I listen to or re-read this book, I find something that I missed."

Michael Raines
Central Home Inspections and Design

"Great book, great people! Just use the products [from Inspector Services Group], listen to the advice in the book, and try not to succeed. Thanks!"

Kevin Sixsmith
Amerispec

"This book helped clarify what I was doing and where I needed to go to get to the next level."

Tony Burk
Accutech Home Inspections, LLC

"When I received the Hungry Home Inspector (first edition), I read it three times in two days. I immediately created a list of items to do that I found in the book. As a result, I did 176 inspections in 2013, 420 in 2014, and I am projecting over 600 in 2015. I attribute a lot of my success to Nathan, his awesome team, and tips I got from this book as well as his second book, Change|Up."

Sheehan Thomson
OnSite Home Inspections

"Nathan- Read your book on the plane ride home! Nice, easy, understandable read. Since I have read the book three times. Having this information is invaluable to running your business!"

Hank Richter
Home Pro Inspections of Rhode Island

"Thanks to the Hungry Home Inspector, I'm getting bored of eating steak all the time...I had to switch to shrimp and lobster!"

Kevin Lucas
KP Home Inspections, LLC

"I have your book and it opened up my mind to a whole new approach to marketing."

David Lightner
Home Pride Home Inspection Services, LLC

"The Hungry Home Inspector could also be titled The Mindset Shift because it is an instrumental piece for any home inspector who is ready to build a home inspection business. Doing a great inspection is the given, it's what you do to wrap that great inspection into a full service product that separates the business owners from those who own their job. This book is a map that sets you on the path to success."

Troy Pappas
Safe House Property Inspections

"Reading this book helped me understand the difference between being a technician and being a business owner. Nothing wrong with either, but it helped me realize I wanted to run a business."

Will Misegades
RedFish Home Inspections

"Before reading this book I was aiming for the stars, but was destined for mediocrity. Nathan's extensive involvement and insight in the industry allow him to destroy the myths that plague it, and obliterate the road blocks. He paved a clear way to success and we have over 260% growth this year over last. I'd actually prefer no other inspector in my market ever reads this book."

Juan Jimenez
A House on a Rock Home Inspections, LLC

"Nathan challenges the reader to go beyond the traditional technician mindset and learn how to make a great living out of one's passion for all that is mechanical and one's passion for sharing knowledge and helping people. The Hungry Home Inspector answers all the what, why, and how to questions that lead you to putting your business in high gear, and receiving all you deserve in this business. Learn the management systems, people skills, and behavioral norms which are now used by the most successful home inspection companies. Nathan is clearly a giant in this rapidly evolving industry, and you need to get on the bandwagon or get left behind!"

Philo Ramos
PRECISE Home Inspections

"The Hungry Home Inspector is a must have! My business was doing well and I felt I was going in the right direction. This book gave me the real ways to grow, become, and act successful. Well written and innovative. All my students are required to read this book!"

Jim Van Loosen
ASAP Home Inspections and Environmental Testing

"Excellent advice and I enjoyed the humor as well. I can't wait to read and learn from your next book [Change|Up]!"

Susan Giuffre
National Property Inspections

"If you just want to be a home inspector and do a few inspections, you don't really need this book. If your goal is to run a home inspection business, and a very successful one, then this book is a must have! Nathan takes you step by step on how to succeed in ways you never thought of or in ways others have probably taught you would never work."

Mark Bateman
PRO SPECT Inspection Services

"As the owner of a multi-inspector firm, I'm here to say that Nathan's book is the E Myth of the home inspection industry."

Jon Bolton
Inspectagator

"The Inspector Services Group is the best! All of the USP's (90-Day Warranty, RecallChek, SewerGard, MoldSafe) and the tips in the book are making a big different to my bottom line."

Ellery Kington
Coastal Home Inspection

"I've known Nathan for years now and his integrity and willingness to help inspectors build their business is to be applauded. I've gained much from this book- even after I chose years ago to utilize many of the products that he provides.

Ron Poteet
Southwest Home Inspection

"I thought the book was a great- a thought provoking read. We will utilize the book as a marketing textbook at our school."

Drew Levy
National Institute of Building Inspectors

"I purchased the book and decided to read it, because when the subject of inspections comes up, I want to be the smartest person in the room. This book may not be liked by many of the traditional home inspectors, many of whom do not think to the future or where the industry is going. This book tells you why and how to overcome that and it is right to the point. Nathan tells it how it is, like it or not. I only hope my competition doesn't follow everything in the book...if I could prevent my competition from reading it I would!"

John Shishilla
Honor Construction and Inspection Service

"I just finished this book and I'm overwhelmed with the quality of the writing. I have a shelf full of books about home inspection, how to do this that and the other. I plan to donate them to all my competitors. I have found all the information I need in one place."

Rory Warren
Warren Home Inspections

"I just finished the book. Awesome! I recommend it for anyone in the home inspection business...except for anyone in the Charlotte market."

Preston Sandlin
Home Inspection Carolina

"The Hungry Home Inspector deciphers the difference between having a job that runs you versus leading a business that runs with systems and people. Be prepared to think bigger, get better, and act bolder as you journey through this book.

Michael Maher
Best Selling Author, The Seven Levels of Communication

Chapter 1
Beginnings

I remember two things distinctly from when I was six years old. The first was a one-time event. I was in my room in Carmel, Indiana. There was a bunk bed and matching dresser and desk, and on top of the desk there were two items- a black and white television, with its own set of rabbit ear antennae, and a standard brown desk lamp.

Having been a ride-along guest on home inspections with my dad, an electrician turned home inspector, I felt very competent in diagnosing the electrical problem I was faced with one day. Sitting alone in my room this fateful afternoon, I was playing the Sega Master System for so long that day turned to dusk, dusk turned to night, and I turned the switch on the back of the lamp but the light didn't come on. I removed the bulb, and checked it out. There may have been a slight rattle, but no significant discoloration, so I started to wonder what could be going on here. The light bulb may or may not be bad, but I didn't know.

So I proceeded to check the light switch that controlled this outlet, it was on. No problem there, and even if there were a problem with that, my parents would certainly inquire why I needed a screwdriver if I went to get one. This would, of course, result in my dad resolving the issue, not me, and that was a scenario I was not willing to accept.

So I put the bulb back in the fixture, thinking maybe I did not turn the switch for those two clicks that it needs to make before it turns on. I knew I had turned it for at least one click, so if I turn it for one more click and then a second click, the light would turn on if the bulb were good at some point. So I turned it one click...nothing. One more click...nothing again.

So now there's only one other possibility, one other variable, before I could be pretty darn certain that this bulb is, in fact, bad. So I removed the bulb, and inserted my right index finger directly into the socket.

This was the first of many times in the decades to follow that I would feel alternating current flow through a finger or hand, something that hardly bothers me today at the right voltage and amp levels, but something about that first time is just really exciting.

When I got back up off the floor, I quickly checked to make sure my arm was the same color and that it had feeling, and then I picked up the light bulb, walked to the other end of the house where part of the garage had been converted into an office, and told my mom with absolute confidence, "This light bulb has gone bad."

It would take something as significant as electrical shock to make the list of things I remember from such a young age as well as that office. The office consisted of a metal desk with a laminate wood top, a typewriter, and files piled up all around the room. The ASHI Code of Ethics was framed neatly and hung on the wall, and then there was that phone. The phone was a constant presence.

That phone gets answered within three rings, period. Why? *If we didn't answer the phone, a competitor would.*

What I couldn't fully understand and really didn't until much later on is that my parents were not home inspectors. That's what they called themselves, sure. That's what they did, of course.

They were not simply home inspectors. They were *business owners*. They were building systems that they could replicate, over and over again.

The rules weren't for them to follow. They were for everyone else to follow. From the way they answered the phone and took an order, to the inspection format and even the standardized comments: "EOPM W/N @ SE CRNR CS," this was the short code that my dad would write on his field form that would then come back to the home office and my mother would type it out: "Evidence of prior moisture was noted at southeast corner of crawl space." It was the start of a system of short codes and standardized notes that remained in use until the day they began using software that allowed them and all of their inspectors to quickly, efficiently, and accurately begin delivering the inspection reports on site. "On-site" is the modern equivalent of the "typed and bound" report of the 80's, when most inspectors were still handwriting their reports. This can be accomplished with many of the more popular reporting programs on the market today- the one they utilized to get it done was Horizon from Carson Dunlop. Until that point, we went from Canon typewriters to FileMaker.

As a teenager I began taking orders, typing reports, and even looking up codes in the NEC and other code books. I later became the marketing manager, even handled complaints and performed miscellaneous inspection duties, never a full inspection by any means- and if you're an inspector reading this book you almost certainly have skills that exceed mine in the technical task of inspecting a home.

After typing around 15,000 inspection reports, booking about as many orders, and handling hundreds of "complaints" (the quotation marks are there on purpose), I've definitely had more customer service and report-writing experience than 99% of inspectors out there and probably dealt with more unusual structural and mechanical situations than most as well. I don't say this to build myself up, but rather to gain credibility. You'd be surprised at how many inspectors truly believe that anyone who isn't walking on a roof or getting in an attic every day has nothing valuable to offer, which couldn't be further from the truth.

By the year 2000, I was running a home warranty company and a construction and development company, simultaneously shortly thereafter.

In 2001, after being fired by my mother three times, I was hired again...sort of. Having run Residential Warranty Services, Inc. successfully, she suggested a product to me for companies like hers to utilize: a 90-Day Warranty.

It was an interesting concept, so we wrote it up and Security Home Inspections (my parent's inspection company) began using it almost immediately. I had no idea at the time that this would be something that would change the home inspection industry forever- but I really knew nothing about the "industry." What I knew came from being in a home inspection business. I grew up around it. I was there when home inspections were incredibly basic and almost everyone doing it was also a contractor of some sort with few exceptions, like my parents. I had been there when they got their first office- a two story, hundred-year-old house built next to the train tracks. I was there when they were the first home inspection company, probably throughout the Midwest, to occupy a commercial office space. I was there when they built a 10,000 square foot office building and expanded their reach to every major metro area throughout the state of Indiana. I was there for the company outings, I was there when they bought a fleet of Ford Rangers, I was there when they hired a uniform service, and when they added health benefits and section 125 health savings accounts, and I was there when my mother worked closely with our state legislators to get inspector licensing passed.

While dinner conversation was frequently clouded by talk of when GFCI outlets became a requirement for installation in the basement of new homes and the proper size of an egress window, more often we talked about business matters like hiring a sales rep and how they should be paid or what the next marketing piece would look like.

So when we started offering a 90-Day Warranty with every inspection from Security Home Inspections, it just made sense. I had answered the phones for years and sold people on using the company, I knew what Security Home Inspections was about, and I also knew that they weren't the cheapest or most available by far. They were in high demand, and getting that client to book eight days in advance and ask for an extension on their inspection response instead of calling the next guy in the phone book required much more than saying that you are a "good inspector." Longevity stands for many things- we've been in business for 25 + years, we have over a dozen full-time inspectors, full-time mold and radon staff, the first in the area to offer color digital photographs, an office you can call any time and get a live person...all sorts of things like that. People like to hear those sorts of things, but none of them are compelling reasons to consider *none other* than Security Home Inspections. All people have to do is pick up the phone, call any inspector in town, and they'll hear them say something like... we're "certified" inspectors, we do a "thorough" inspection, we offer a color digital photo page with every report, etc. With the 90-Day Warranty, there was suddenly a dilemma the other inspectors couldn't handle, because their level of service and product offerings had never really been called into question. The client would call, ask if they offered a warranty, and the responses would do nothing but convince the client even more that they should go with Security Home Inspections. A few of my favorite responses;

"No we don't."

"That's not a part of our [minimum] inspection standards per [fill in name of organization here]."

"I can't tell you anything about what will happen to the house in the future, I'm just there to inspect."

"But we're cheaper."

It was one of Security Home Inspections' best growth years ever- not only by volume, but also by inspection revenue as well. Prices were increased that year, and the total number of inspection appointments went over 7,000. Their market share was around 22%. In a marketplace with about 80 other licensed firms...you do the math.

It wasn't long before other inspectors were inquiring about the warranties, and that was when I got my first taste of the real world, so to speak. An inspector would call, ask me some questions, figure out I knew what I was talking about, and since at the time I was dealing mostly with local people, I would offer to meet at their office, except they didn't have one.

This was mind blowing to me.

How can you have a business and not have an office? The more I learned, the more I was convinced that my parents' business was quite exceptional. Most inspectors don't have an office staff, don't have multiple inspectors, and don't have marketing reps. They wish they could afford health insurance but it's nearly impossible without a group plan.

As it turns out, Security Home Inspections was uniquely situated at the front of the herd and had become about the 5th largest single location inspection company in the country, and by far the largest in the Midwest.

Now, before we go much further, I want to make sure to make some things perfectly clear;

1. There's nothing wrong with small! In fact, there are a lot of great things about it, so don't be turned off if you don't want to be that 5+ inspector firm because that is NOT what this book is about.
2. This is not a sales pitch. For those who know me, they know I work with a lot of home inspectors. I work with mostly successful home inspectors, as the unsuccessful ones or the ones with the unsuccessful mindset won't ever consider even looking at many of our products like RecallChek, 90-Day Warranties, SewerGard, MoldSafe, InspectorLab, or The Alarm Leads Program. Trying to sell you stuff in a book would not only be lame, but it would

be ineffective. I'd rather make you more successful and give you that successful mindset. Then if and when *you* ultimately make the decision to work with us on some level, it will be because you decided to and because it was a good business decision, *not* because you were "sold" something.

3. There are many ways to accomplish the same thing. Spin was invented for a reason, and when I say "spin," I mean the kind of spin that cable news channels put on political issues. Spin should absolutely be used in the way you sell yourself. You should always be confident and *know* you have the best product. Here's a great example: some inspectors deliver reports on-site, others deliver next day. You can give clients the sense that convenience is key, and that you're good enough and have the systems necessary to deliver the report on site where others fall short. Or you could promote the virtues of reviewing the report thoroughly to make sure the client is taken care of by releasing the report the next day. Either way works pretty well when executed properly.

4. *Nothing* in this book negates the need for knowledgeable and ethical home inspectors. In all my travels, meeting and speaking to literally thousands of inspectors, it never ceases to amaze me how many believe that good marketing equals haphazard inspections. A few stubborn, unfortunate, self-sabotaging individuals will likely read into this book something nefarious that they conjured up themselves. I am of the opinion that 99% of inspectors out there are really good people and well-intentioned, and most of them do a great inspection. Show me an inspector pointing to another and saying, "That guy doesn't focus on quality like I do!" and I'll show you an inspector who is either A.) Lying to himself, B.) Getting his butt kicked and not making the money he wants (or needs) to make, or C.) Both. If you don't

believe me, take a look at Home Inspection University (www.HomeInspectionUniversity.com). Most of the courses there are all about mechanical and structural systems, the courses are all overseen by Mike Casey, and a free trial of the service is available to every inspector in North America.

So let's just clear the air right now. I don't know a single home inspector in North America who wakes up in the morning, puts on his uniform, steps out onto his porch and thinks to himself, "You know, today I aim to provide poor service, perform my duties unethically, and miss as many defects as possible." Sounds silly doesn't it? It's the myth of the "bad" inspector. I've publicly offered to hire a team to go undercover and bust the "bad" inspector. No one has taken me up on this offer to date, as we are releasing this 2nd Edition of *The Hungry Home Inspector* in 2015. If you'd like to take me up on this offer, go to www.HomeInspectionForum.net!

Many inspectors pride themselves on doing a thorough job, not realizing somehow that just about everybody in this business has the same level of pride in their own inspections. There are levels of anality, but at the end of the day inspection reports differ mostly in our own minds.

They (the inspectors that focus only on quality) put out fliers and business cards that say, "I'm a good home inspector," and then proceed to list all the home systems they inspect, which was a novel concept in the late 70's and even through the 80's, when agents and buyers alike really didn't know what a home inspection was.

Then there are the other home inspectors, the ones that ignore their competition, create a message that can be understood and appreciated by home buyers and agents alike, and they give clients tangible reasons to choose them. You can't turn around without seeing their message. They have logo-ridden trucks and business cards with content on both sides. You can find them weekly at sales meetings talking to agents, delivering fliers and other marketing material. When you call them, they answer the phone consistently and when you ask them why someone should get a home inspection with them, they give you an answer, an actual answer. What you won't hear them say is "because we do a thorough inspection." (The actual answer is the central focus of this book.)

It's the difference between being hungry for more and just being hungry, and that is what this book is about.

Chapter 2
The Journey

It's tough to get a sense of what's going on somewhere without actually being there yourself. You'd think that everyone in Nashville wears a cowboy hat and boots and loves country music if you watched the Country Music Awards on CMT and if country wasn't your thing, you'd have no interest in going. You might be surprised to know that downtown Nashville is quite stunning. Walking between the skyscrapers, on rolling hills of concrete and grates, there are phenomenal restaurants and clubs. There's a B.B. King restaurant with live blues every night. There's a Coyote Ugly- that place where the bartenders dance on the bar every 15 minutes or so and yes, it's the same Coyote Ugly featured in that movie, just a different location.

They have a huge music venue downtown, across Broadway from an incredible convention center connected to a large hotel. Two of the new skyscrapers downtown, built in the last decade, are high-end condominiums with a style that seems very Chicago or even Manhattan. The only country music related stuff I see when I'm down there is along one strip of Broadway- 9 or 10 bars with live music and a couple of discount boot and hat stores mixed in.

If you've experienced downtown Nashville, you know what I'm talking about. If you haven't, then you don't. You may have a different idea of what it's like, but no matter what that idea is, it won't truly match reality until you go there.

Much the same can be said about success - which is why we are starting this book with a journey- the journey I took over the last three decades but mostly in the last fifteen years- because I could tell you in less than five pages of text exactly what you need to do to be successful in the home inspection business (In fact, I did in the book *Change|Up*, in a chapter entitled "No Excuses"). If we were face to face, it might take less than three minutes. Most of it would have nothing at all to do with any of my products or services. I *could* do that...

BUT THAT WON'T WORK.

It's been proven time and time again. I attended an event in North Carolina, the NCLHIA (North Carolina Licensed Home Inspector Association), and it was a great experience. I probably picked up no less than 45 new clients, which is slightly higher than my usual percentage based on the number of people there. Why was it higher? I had been invited to speak the day before the event, along with Dominic Maricic of Home Inspector Pro, Dan Huber of Inspection Support Network, and a few others. Those in attendance listened to great presentations, and accounted for the majority of our signups that weekend. The other inspectors didn't sign up at nearly the same frequency.

There was one moment that was the "proof" I speak of above- the proof that simply giving you the short answers to increasing your revenue levels and overall client satisfaction won't work- and I have a witness to this. A home inspector came up to my booth and started talking to me. He wasn't doing a lot of inspections, he felt real estate agents were in the way and he wanted to go around them (a topic we will cover at length later on, but needless to say...he was wrong!) He was looking for some advice on how to do that. Dan Huber, the witness, looked on with curiosity as I proceeded to tell this particular inspector about how agents in his area largely weren't the problem, but that in fact, he was. He was real estate transaction Kryptonite- for several reasons. Not because he did a "thorough" inspection, not because of what he found or didn't find on his inspections, but because of the way he worded defects and his overall attitude toward agents. Some things he mentioned in his report weren't defects at all.

What inspectors don't realize when they approach the vendor hall at these conventions is that most of the vendors there are seasoned professionals who have been around the business as long as or longer than most of the inspectors. As I'm writing this book, we (The Inspector Services Group and Residential Warranty Services, Inc.) are involved in more real estate transactions in a month than the average home inspector could accomplish in over 400 years in the business. That's not an exaggeration. If anything, I'm underestimating for believability, but even at that level we see just about everything in any given month.

My point being, you can get some great advice from vendors and you'll be surprised at how many vendors don't really "sell" anything at these events. Most are well-established in the industry, and many of them will tell you that the reason they go to events is to keep connected to their clients and deliver support for their products. When we set up booths at events, and I speak for most vendors in the industry, we have no expectation that sales on the day of the show will meet or exceed our expenses.

At that event in North Carolina, the inspector I was talking to had some serious foundational issues related to his business and I wanted to help him fix that. He didn't want to hear it, he wanted a quick fix and to move on. I helped him as much as I could, then helped him with the "moving on" part and told him to come back and see me in a year or so when his way still isn't working and when he's ready to try it another way. I don't need (or want) someone out there attached to our brand who is hateful or holds disdain for those who refer most all of the inspections that ever happen (real estate agents) and shows it in everything he does.

A month later, he decided to open up and try it "the other way." It worked out great, but he had to take that journey to discover why he needed to change and how he was going to do it without losing his identity. You have to be yourself, just not the self that sabotages your own business and seemingly *hates* money. *My editor who works full time for a major business and finance publication had crossed out the phrase "hates money" and indicated I should change it because in her words, "No one hates money!" Then I had her read two pages of an inspector forum online and she later admitted, "Apparently, there are people who hate money."*

I'm hoping your journey is just a few pages in a book rather than another month of lackluster sales and struggles.

So let's start that journey together, and I'm going to go back several years. Remember at this point that I've been around the business; I think I know everything about it, and I get a call from a friend of my family. He used to run a large inspection company and was in a mastermind group where a dozen of the largest inspection companies in North America exchanged thoughts and ideas with my parents for decades and was running a coaching group now.

As you can imagine, I'm pretty skeptical at this point. If I hadn't known this man for many years, I would have hung up the phone within ten seconds of hearing the word "coaching."

His name is Mike Crow, and he invited me to one of his mastermind groups, this one being held in California.

I wasn't told what to expect, I wasn't told to bring anything, just to show up.

I had no idea walking into that room that by the time I walked out, I would develop lifelong friendships, all home inspection company owners from around the country. We spent three days locked in a conference room of a hotel, talking about all sorts of things. Much of it is proprietary and confidential and I can't share it, but some of it is common-sense marketing stuff we should all be doing and just need a reminder of at times. Mike regularly shares a lot of these things on the public stage.

It was brought to my attention at that meeting by a few of the attendees that there was a huge void in the market. They had heard of my one-year home warranties I sold through real estate agents, knew I did 90-Day Home Inspection Warranties for my parents' company, and wondered if I could do these warranties for them as well.

My response: "Sure, let me look into it."

Usually, I respond with a very quick "YES!" when someone wants to pay for my services, but in this case there were a lot of variables I had to deal with. Various state regulatory issues were the biggest things on my mind. What the attendees in that room didn't know at the time was that the other players in the 90-Day Warranty market weren't just disappointing them on the service and marketing side, they were about to be hit with notifications from multiple states (i.e., Florida, Wisconsin, and The Commonwealth of Virginia) regarding their lack of compliance with those states' laws. What it came down to was that they had no idea these regulations existed because they weren't professionals from the warranty industry. They didn't even have insurance backgrounds. One of the players was super-strong in home inspection, the other was a small venture firm whose largest undertaking appeared to be bison farming. There's only a slight difference between running an agricultural operation and managing risk. In risk management you have to create actuarial models, develop processes, and most importantly, comply with regulations.

A few months later, we had released the RWS 90-Day Inspector Warranty Program nationwide. We started calling, e-mailing, and mailing promotions to home inspection companies. We booked conferences, hired a manager for the operation, and for about four months or so the business was pretty easy to run. The first 300 inspectors or so were easy to convince. They "got it."

"You want to offer a warranty with your home inspections?"

"Yes! That would be awesome!"

And it was awesome. We helped this first group of clients with scripting, customized brochures, and getting the word out. They were using the 90-Day Warranty to separate themselves from the competition in a very real way. They offered a warranty, the competition didn't.

A majority of these companies were multi-inspector firms, the kind I grew up around. They had systems in place, they marketed constantly, and they understood how to inspect thoroughly, the way they had all been taught when they got into the business. At the same time they respected the position they had in the real estate transaction, and respected the role of the agent referring them in the transaction.

This is probably the most difficult concept for most inspectors to grasp: the real estate agent as a referring *customer*. There's often confusion about who is a *client* and who is a *customer*.

The key difference is this: Without clients, you're not doing any business, and the way to obtain clients is to have a line of customers ready to supply you with business.

This is kind of a difficult thing to do when you have no respect for those who have the potential to make you or break you. There's an entire chapter in this book about how Web pioneers get slaughtered. The chapter isn't what you probably think, I'm not *against* good Web marketing. You should have a good Web site (actually multiple, see www.UltimateInspectorWebsites.com), you can buy ads and do some SEO (Search Engine Optimization), and you can do some consumer direct marketing to supplement your business. The key word being "supplement."

We very quickly ran out of inspectors who ran their businesses professionally and competitively, or at least on the level that they could grasp the concepts we were promoting easily. It became increasingly difficult to convert inspectors into clients and we had to make a change.

The realization had set in...

We knew nothing of the home inspection industry. It was not full of business owners. It was full of home inspectors- that were great at inspecting.

Chapter 3
The Technician Mindset

In the spring of 2012, on my weekly radio show on FOX News, I had an author by the name of Micheal E. Gerber as a guest. We had an hour-long chat about the *Technician Mindset*. Michael is a big deal, like a *really* big deal. With seven million + books sold, every major business magazine has given him huge credit for his advice to small business owners, and he's been a *New York Times* best-selling author many times over.

Micheal's book series, *The E-Myth*, is all about the "Entrepreneurial Myth." I highly recommend reading the book, because although it's written for a general audience, it may as well have "Home Inspector" stamped on the front cover.

We are, with notable exceptions of course, an industry full of technicians that are in business for ourselves. Most inspectors are operating as a one-man shop, working every day to get orders next week in order to go out, do some inspections, make some money, and repeat the process. The fact that the clients make the checks out to us and the fact that we don't have health insurance, a retirement plan, or regular work hours and paid vacations is what defines many inspectors as entrepreneurs. You can add that many in the industry have little protection themselves personally from liabilities, both financial and legal, that the "company" incurs.

Why is it that the home inspection industry seems to be so fragmented? Why is it that the average home inspection *company* performs only about 200 inspections annually, with a *gross* revenue of less than $60,000.00?

More importantly, why is it that most inspectors don't want to do 1,000 inspections or more per year? Why is it that home inspectors don't want to make more than $60,000.00 per year?

I've tested this theory out more than a dozen times. The first time was at an ASHI chapter meeting. I had an inspector, Tony Smith from Iowa, come up to my booth and start talking to me about how great business was. He asked if I had anything more to offer him in the way of marketing advice, and wondered why I wasn't speaking at the event. I said, "Tony, if you ask any inspector in this room what the most important thing is in their business, I'd say making money wouldn't even make it to the top ten."

He said, "You're wrong! Everybody knows that profitability is the most important thing to running a business, without it you don't have a business!"

I pulled up Microsoft Word on my projector and said, "Okay, let's give this a shot."

It was a break, inspectors were grabbing donuts and coffee, and they were walking up. Tony stood there as I asked ten inspectors in a row what the most important thing to them was in their business.

The first one came up and said, "I would say being very well-educated about home systems."

I typed it up on the screen, agreed, and commended him on his principles.

Tony said as the first guy walked away, "Well, that's just one..."

Next inspector walked up...same question. The response was basically "doing a thorough inspection". Then another inspector said "liability." Then another said "being respected by my peers."

Seven more inspectors came by, gave similar answers, and we kept a list. I saw an inspector I knew who had a multi-inspector firm and I waved him over, asked the same question, and he said without hesitation, "Duh! Making money!"

It was number 11 on the list. Tony's eyes were wide open, and he shook his head as we had another conversation about how inspectors would generally rather hear mechanical theory on how a toilet flushes than anything that makes them look like an actual business that markets to those evil, evil...Real Estate Agents!

So you really think you want to make more than $60,000 per year? Is that so?

Well, how many *pure* business books did you read last year? How many marketing seminars did you attend? How many times in the last year have you gone to a real estate agent, the source of almost all referrals for home inspections, and asked them what would make the home inspection process better or easier for all involved?

Maybe I'm being hard on you for no reason. Maybe you do all these things.

Most inspectors do just that: they inspect. They inspect, and then they go home, and then they put together their reports. They send out their reports. They take very good care of their clients...and there's nothing wrong with that, it's just a misnomer to call it "being in business for yourself" if you don't have systems that make it easy, systems that make the process repeatable and duplicable, and a platform that could be run by anyone else with the skill set of a typical home inspector. In other words, if your business can't be sold and transferred for big bucks...it's not a business.

Let me give you some examples of the *Technician Mindset*.

- "I'm the only one who can do my kind of inspection."

- "I don't offer clients anything other than a good inspection."

- "I work for the client, and I don't market to those agents. They're not my client."

I could go on and on...but why do that when we can tear these examples apart!

"I'm the only one who can..." Stop! Why would you ever create a process that only *you* could do? Is there any better way to guarantee you'll retire with exactly the amount of money you have in the bank at that time?

The fact is, whether you are planning on making good money and taking vacations and giving yourself a break from doing two or three inspections a day by some point in your 50's, or if you're planning on taking it easy from the start and don't have any inclination to manage people, either way there is no reason to create a process "only you" could do.

This is classic technician mindset combined with mistaking yourself for an entrepreneur when you're really an *inventor* or an innovator or both...with a hobby. I know this disease well, because even though my dad is incredibly business-minded, creates systems and has more than a dozen inspectors and probably 20+ employees at any given time, he's still a technician and an inventor at heart. If it weren't for my mother, the inspection process would be complex and convoluted in all likelihood.

Remember when infrared cameras first hit the scene, and the only available ones cost over $20,000.00? Yep, my dad bought two and he'd play with them. He gave one to another *inventive technician* who worked for him for more than 20 years, he took it home and started shooting everything in the house figuring out long before any of these IR training companies came around what all they could do with this new technology.

If you've ever seen something on TV or in *Popular Mechanics* and thought to yourself, "I invented that years ago!" – You're prone to making processes complicated. Recognize this; recognize that it is not a strength unfettered. By the way, if you subscribe to *Popular Mechanics* you fit the bill whether you've seen one of your inventions in there or not.

"I don't offer clients anything other than a good inspection." You'll hear it soon enough if you haven't said it yourself. The sad part is that this isn't just something they say to make themselves look "ethical," this is their entire marketing plan.

The *everything else* inferred in the statement is one of two things;

1. Ancillary Services

2. USP's (Unique Selling Propositions)

The ancillary services they don't offer might include termite, radon, water testing, mold testing, well and septic inspection, pool, spa, etc. Maybe they don't believe Radon exists, perhaps they feel Mold is a conspiracy, pool inspections may be beyond their abilities, who knows.

Inspectors who avoid doing these services generally do so thinking they are somehow a more "pure" inspector. "I don't inspect pools because I'm not a pool guy." "I don't check for termites because I'm not a termite guy." "I don't test for mold because I can see mold." Basically I'm an inspector and that's it. My abilities and desire to make money are both equally limited.

What's worse is that inspectors will actually avoid these easy moneymakers that truly benefit clients like the plague while they dive head first into the deep end of infrared cameras and even energy audits that have proven to be largely nothing burgers.

It can't be rationalized, so don't try to figure it out. Why would anyone *not* want to be the guy who offers pool inspections? More money, bigger houses...by the way, probably the easiest part of the inspection. But that's how they run their business, not as a business at all.

The USP's (Unique Selling Propositions) are things like guarantees, warranties, checking for recalls with RecallChek, offering agents marketing tools, SewerGard, MoldSafe, giving clients discount coupons and rebates on products and services they'll need as a new homeowner, or a home manual like The

Ultimate Home Book. Many inspectors with the technician mindset like to call these things "gimmicks," and when you hear this from an inspector you can be sure of two things;

- This inspector is on the low end of the income range for home inspection company owners.

- He's getting his butt kicked by one of his competitors offering something "gimmicky" and resents the way the world is headed.

He longs for the good old days when putting your number in the phone book and your name on a Website and your business card on the corkboard at Home Depot got you enough calls from people who didn't know who to call that you could make a living.

"I work for the client...not the agent!" This is the one where you have to read between the lines and hear the real message: "I don't market."

All inspectors realize, and rightfully so, that yes, we have a responsibility to the client. So whom are you preaching to? Whom are you trying to convince of what?

Your obligation to the home buyer or client isn't unique to you at all. You're really just driving home the point that you don't care for real estate agents. You probably think they don't care for you either.

You're probably right. So let's fix it.

Chapter 4
Inconvenient Truths

It's inconvenient that most people need a mortgage. It's built into our system now, no turning back.

Oh, wait! It's a great thing that the home mortgage exists! If we didn't have mortgages, where would we be? A lot smaller houses, that's for sure...and probably far fewer of them.

Even with mortgages that had huge down payments and were done locally and had five-year balloon payments, the world was very different. Take 20% of the mortgage ability off the top and we're back to the days when grandma lived in the den and the kids stayed home until they married.

It's an inconvenient truth that mortgages exist because of the regulations that come with them. Appraisals are a nightmare today. Approvals can be yanked at the last moment and our bank-owned real estate inventory is truly problematic for our country to this day, even with a fairly decent real estate recovery over the last five years.

They're also inconvenient for real estate agents.

Mortgage guidelines, federal regulations, and the Real Estate Settlement Procedures Act make the agent's job very defined, frustratingly so.

They represent their client, whether it be a buyer or a seller. It's a tough situation to deal with when you have a buyer who's made an offer on the property, it was accepted, and then the appraisal comes in low. What happens now? They have to try to argue with the appraiser, make their case for the value to someone who thinks they know a lot more than the agent does. Or they have to convince the buyer to come up with more cash, or they have to convince the seller to accept a lower price, or a combination of the two- they may even be back to the drawing board or cut their commissions.

But that's the sandbox they have to play in. No real estate agent or company or organization thinks that they invented the process. They can add their nuances, maybe some USP's, but they've learned to adapt the process to the mortgages that nearly every transaction is tied to.

For as much criticism of real estate agents as there is from some home inspectors, the *inconvenient truth* this chapter is focused on is that many home inspectors have a bigger sense of entitlement than agents do.

It's true.

How many times have you heard a group of inspectors talking about the home inspection process and how it relates to the purchase agreement (or "purchase contract")?

Never.

I speak to literally thousands of home inspectors annually, over 10,000 to date, and I'll openly ask the question, "Does anyone here have a copy of a purchase contract?". The answer is always no.

Successful home inspectors realize that the real estate transaction, the agents, and the purchase agreement are their best friends, even if they're a necessary evil. I've actually always liked the agents I deal with, but I can certainly see why inspectors might not take the same view at all times.

Think of it this way: the real estate transaction is a small island, and while it's in progress the inhabitants are you, the agents, the sellers, and the buyers. Tropical Storm "Mortgage Approval" is heading west towards your position and it's picking up speed as it's hitting warm water full of objections, appraisal issues, and inspection problems...luckily we have this Hurricane Shelter called the Purchase Agreement, cool heads, cooperation, and...uh oh. The inspector just lit the Hurricane Shelter on fire.

Many inspectors will not appreciate the severity of my analogy. They'll say that they're not a part of the real estate transaction. This is coincidentally exactly what most agents in their market probably say about them as well. We found common ground!

There are many inspectors who believe that their job is completely separate from the real estate transaction. I'm convinced that some of them may even believe they invented the inspection process.

What they fail to realize is that the inspection is *defined* in the purchase agreement. No ifs, ands, or buts about it.

Do yourself a *huge* favor and get a blank purchase agreement from your local real estate board. If they won't help you, talk to an agent. Somehow, get your hands on one.

Find the section regarding the inspection response. Read it.

What did it say?

Did it say anything about the buyer being able to ask the seller to replace something that is perfectly operational simply because it is old?

No!

Let's think about this one for a second. In an earlier chapter, I mentioned an inspector who was "Real Estate Agent Kryptonite." I told you he had some foundational issues in his business, and the way he was reporting some things were creating problems. He said agents didn't like him, which didn't surprise me at all.

You see, he had either no knowledge or no respect for the real estate transaction. Forget the agents for the moment; let's talk about the client, the one we're all obligated to.

The client signed a contract to purchase the property- and within that contract, very clearly defined, was the timing for and subject matter that could be contained within an inspection response. It also had a completely, totally separate section that discussed operational but older appliances and components. It was the section about home warranties.

Thirty years ago, inspectors were largely defining the home inspection industry as it was still in its infancy. The standards varied enormously from company to company, and a large contingency of home inspectors became accustomed to making statements about older equipment suggesting that they were "defunct" or in need of replacement or "beyond their useful life expectancy." Even twenty years ago, there was certainly a place for this tactic when it came to furnaces, air conditioners, and water heaters, but not today. Old water heaters are addressed in the purchase agreement and don't require any predictive statements from the home inspector.

It's not a point that's up for debate; it's a fact that is in writing in a legal document in every real estate transaction throughout the U.S. and Canada.

This rule does NOT apply to roof coverings, as an example. A roof that is gone is gone, whether it's leaking or not. Call it. The rule only applies to mechanical items that fall under extended warranties available to home buyers.

Who are you to say when a water heater needs to be replaced? If it's old, find an issue with it. Run it a little extra, see if you can get it to go lukewarm or cold. Call any actual defect on it you can, but don't try to define the home inspection as something distinct and separate from the defined process outlined in the purchase agreement. If you try to do so, you will succeed, and you won't be a part of the real estate transaction.

If you had presented these facts to as many inspectors as I have, you would know that there will be a guy who stands up and makes a statement that goes something like this:

"I'm not going to do a walk-through inspection for cheap so that I can get business from agents. If they want someone to gloss over defects they can hire someone else!"

It makes me want to ask if they have a hearing problem, or just simply don't understand English. Maybe they were dropped on their head frequently as a child.

Who said gloss over defects? Who said walk-through inspection? Who said *cheap?*

Nobody did.

When an inspector has defined his position as being *against* real estate agents he has also defined his business as being non-conducive to the real estate transaction, and that is why he does fewer inspections than he should. That's why he doesn't make as much money as he should.

It's much easier to be thorough when you're prepared to be hated for being so. Being thorough and respected for it is much more difficult, and some inspectors just aren't up to the task, *it's scary to them.* It takes finesse and a little bit of salesmanship.

Chapter 5

The Myth of the Bad Inspector

In late 2010, we launched a new feature for *RecallChek*. Today it's the most utilized e-mail marketing platform in the real estate industry, and basically, without telling you too much, it's a feature where the client is automatically enrolled in an on-going e-mail campaign with his real estate agent getting the credit. The agent's name goes at the top of the newsletter, the inspector's name at the bottom, with a "Monthly Maintenance Minute" and it's all done for you. It's easy, which is a big part of why it's been a huge success.

As we do with many features, we launched the concept via a Webinar. This allows us to get instant feedback from clients and prospective clients, and the Webinar environment allows us to hear objections from inspectors. It prepares us to talk to other inspectors.

I was explaining the new feature, how to utilize it in sales presentations, and I gave a specific example of how it had already been used by The Elite Group in California to get more sales presentations, and how it was opening doors that had been closed for years.

Out of nowhere, an inspector made a comment via the chat feature about how he was familiar with The Elite Group, and how they did "really bad inspections." It was not a particularly unique comment; I get negative ones about inspectors all the time from their competition.

But this comment didn't come from California. This statement was made by a home inspector on the East Coast.

Usually I just let the ignorant comments go, but in this particular case I went ahead and brought the comment up publicly.

What this inspector didn't know is that I had spent time with each of Elite Group's 35 home inspectors, spent more than a full week in their office, and worked directly with their inspection manager for years on quality control. They were also the first major home inspection company in the country to include *RecallChek* in their base inspection- only after a thorough discussion and market testing.

In other words, I know a lot about this company and I'm happy I do. They're the #1 inspection company in the country by volume from a single location. Nobody else serves more than 15,000 clients annually.

I went ahead and gave this inspector on the Webinar a chance to say his piece. I read his comment, didn't use his name, and then offered to unmute his microphone so he could enlighten us about how "bad" The Elite Group was personally. He didn't have a microphone on his computer (big surprise).

So I responded to his comment after reading it to the webinar attendees;

"You know guys, this is the kind of bullcrap that really hurts our industry. Here's an inspector, more than 2,000 miles away from another one, saying that an inspection company doesn't do a good, thorough inspection when he likely has no idea at all what's involved in an Elite Group inspection. He's almost certainly never seen one of their reports, never even possibly heard from one of their clients, it would be the same as me saying that he's an incompetent idiot and a walking liability, which he could very well be, I don't know, which is why I don't say it. I tend to think he's probably a good inspector, and I only hope he's as good as The Elite Group. Just to set the record straight, my company issues a 90-Day Warranty on every inspection The Elite Group does, and they have one of the lowest claim rates of *any* inspection company in North America. They're insured to a level most inspectors can't even afford and they haven't had a claim for as long as I've known them. Not only do I see their inspection reports but also I've personally been to an inspection with every single one of their more than 35 inspectors, and I would say they do as good a job as anybody out there, if not better. Oh, and by the way, I send out a *RecallChek* report to every single one of their clients and I have a folder in my *Outlook* full of responses from satisfied clients marked "The Elite Group". So unless you can show me 50+ e-mails from satisfied clients in your business from just last week alone, I'd suggest we take some important lessons from big, successful home inspection companies- because, let's be honest, the *only* reason this guy could have possibly had this opinion of The Elite Group is because he got it from another inspector who's in the same market as The Elite Group and he is getting his butt kicked."

Yes, our Webinars are very entertaining at times, but they are a "No B.S. Zone."

That night was the first time I truly understood how powerful the myth of the "bad" inspector was. If you ask most inspectors what a "bad" inspector is, they'll likely start rattling off things like, "Inspectors who don't follow the Standards of Practice," or "Inspectors who do walk-through inspections."

You won't hear things like, "Inspectors who put out inspection reports that agents can't decipher."

You will hear, "Inspectors that miss things."

Well, show me an inspector who says he's never missed anything, and I'll show you the biggest liar in the room. We've all missed something. I'm sure that even in this second edition of this book there is a simple spelling error.

This is why I have a slightly different definition for a "bad" inspector. I think an inspector who doesn't have a profitable business model is a bad inspector. I think an inspector who doesn't have the resources to resolve issues when they arise and provide a great life for their family is a "bad" inspector. I think an inspector who refuses to fix a $1,000 issue for a client referred by an agent who refers them $5,000 in business every year is making a bad business decision and is, in fact, a "bad" inspector. I think an inspector who thinks it's a good idea to offer the minimum service they have to and worries more about liability than growth is a "bad" inspector.

As an industry, we don't focus on the health of our businesses, but rather on how well one inspects.

Nobody goes into home inspection for the money. They do it because they know about things mechanical and structural, they do it because they love inspecting, and almost nobody walks into the business with zero experience.

As I write this 2nd Edition, I have more than 4,500 home inspectors on one of my programs. I see their reports, I hear from their clients, and I've worked with their insurance companies. I can't name you an inspector I know whom I wouldn't have inspect my own house.

If the way you promote yourself is that you're a "good, thorough inspector" and you are on a quest to save people from getting a bad inspection...I have an idea for you. This may be the best investment you could ever possibly make;

Get an inspection.

It may sound crazy, but this line of thinking that you are going to succeed because you are a good inspector and "everyone else sucks" is toxic. It will cost you literally hundreds of thousands of dollars over the remainder of your career.

So spend the $200-$500 now, and get a home inspection. Find a friend or family member, someone you can trust but has a different last name that has preferably purchased a home or several homes. Inspect their house, the same way you inspect every day. Produce a report. Then have your friend hire the other inspector to inspect the house. Have them tell the inspector that they are represented by a real estate agent, that they are currently renting the home and have made an offer to purchase it.

When you're done, put the inspections side by side, in front of your friend, but with all identifying marks taped over. Just sit there, listen as they go through the reports.

Of course there are exceptions, but I would say more than 99% of the time this experiment will result in both reports having every single major item ($500-$1000+ expense to repair) in common.

If every inspector did this, the myth of the "bad" inspector would be dispelled, and maybe we'd stop debating the proper way to install a toilet and start the discussion of how we take inspections to the next level. I'm not just referring to things like warranties, guarantees, RecallChek, SewerGard, MoldSafe, or anything else we offer. I'm referring to things like new ways we could use IR and market it as a service, extended service and support for clients, and systems to keep in touch with past clients. Real business initiatives.

Maybe we could actually have the discussion as an industry of how we truly work better with real estate agents. How more of us could become a part of the real estate transaction without losing our integrity, our identity, or our desire to be thorough in everything we do.

Since we released the 1st edition of this book, we started the Home Inspection & Real Estate Message Board to do just that. Go to www.HomeInspectionForum.net.

Chapter 6
Pioneers Get Slaughtered

The first time I saw Dominic Maricic at a convention in Las Vegas, I had not heard of him before. I hadn't heard of Home Inspector Pro. All I knew was that here's a guy with Chuck Taylors, glasses, slim fit jeans, and a t-shirt selling something to inspectors. He was selling software, but talking about Google, and he was going on and on and on... and the inspectors weren't leaving!

I had to interrupt him to introduce myself.

That's Dominic's style. You go up to his booth, ask him anything about Website design, Google rankings, or any other related topic and he will talk about it until you decide to walk away. Maybe you're a client of his, maybe you're not, it doesn't matter. He's going to educate you.

He's the opposite of what you would think inspectors would gravitate towards, but they come in droves.

Why?

His stuff works. It just works.

There are a multitude of ways to get your Website up and going, and there are even some other great providers in the industry- but I see Dominic as *the* catalyst behind the inspection industry's Web domination. If you're not going to get a website from www.UltimateInspectorWebsites.com, get one (or three) from Dominic!

Typical home inspections run around $300. The typical homebuyer purchases one house every seven years. More than 80% of homebuyers will go with the first inspector recommended by their real estate agent. That leaves less than 20% (and probably less than 10%) of around five million homebuyers each year in the U.S. and Canada who will be shopping for a home inspector, and while many of them will do an Internet search, it's still an incredibly small market.

In fact, I would challenge you to find any industry with as many participants in the Internet marketing game. Search just about any city on Google, combine that with "home inspection", "home inspector", or "inspection," and you're going to find both paid ads at the top of the page as well as natural results that lead directly to an inspector's Website. Pages and pages of them. Do the same search for appliance repair, all you get is responses from Yelp and Service Magic and the like. There are probably 20 times as many appliance repairs as home inspections each year, and nearly all of those homeowners are shopping for a service provider. That makes the Internet market in appliance repair more than 80 times as big as home inspection yet home inspectors are light years ahead.

Vendors like Dominic make it easy, and my advice is simple. Spend some money; get your Website up and ranked on Google. Also, *don't rely on your Website and client referrals to be your sole sources of business or even a major portion of your business.*

The problem with Web sites that drive some inspection business is that they drive "some" business. They offer a glimmer of hope to inspectors that don't want to put the hard work into establishing a real estate-transaction-friendly product, and don't want to actually get out and do the hard work of marketing their service. Let the Website do all the work.

This is where the Web pioneers in our industry are getting hurt *big time*. Every inspector is capable of doing 500, 600, even 1,000 inspections per year and make really good money doing it. Once you get to a certain point, you can create systems that work and start hiring inspectors. It's called running a business. But if you get your share of the small amount of inspections out there being booked as a result of Web searches, you get a distorted view of what success looks like.

Fact: There is not an inspection company in the country doing $1 million+ in revenue with any significant portion of it coming from their Website.

It doesn't mean that these companies don't have Websites. Doesn't mean they don't pay for ads or spend money and resources on getting ranked on Google. Several of them are dominantly ranked in their market.

It just means that they don't let the rare homebuyer who doesn't trust their agent's recommendations define their business.

There are exceptional stories of home inspectors who have absolutely mastered the art of luring in these paranoid exceptions. I'm truly impressed, but at the same time I feel sorry for some of them who don't realize that by making these statements on their Website and even at the inspection about how clients should trust them over anyone recommended by their agent is really just alienating them from real estate offices and making them look really bad. They're the same kind of inspectors who inadvertently say to buyers every once in awhile "I wouldn't buy this house!" (Even if they didn't use those words precisely.)

It's the marketing equivalent of a bear trap in home inspection, and chatter on the inspection forums and at local inspector events multiplies its effects.

"I got an inspection yesterday from my Website...and I didn't have to worry about impressing the damn real estate agent!"

Misguided statements like this make the inspector the envy of his peers, or at least some of them. The statement should really be better qualified or expanded. It would make things more honest, because nobody will speak up and ask the necessary questions, the business questions that should be asked. For instance, how many of these appointments are you booking per day? How many agent referrals do you get per day? (The answers to these questions are incredibly unimpressive)

The really good inspection business owners out there don't rely on Web promotion. They know that 80%+ of their business should come from agent referrals. The other 20% that comes from their Website is just gravy.

Chapter 7
A True Marketing Message

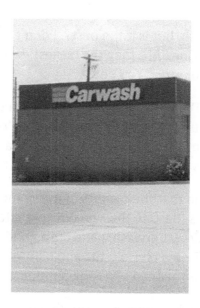

From Baltimore to L.A., Chicago to Dallas, everywhere I go there are car washes within a few miles. Some of them are automatic machines, others are spray hoses you need a pocketful of quarters to operate. Then there are some that have people who dry your car off by hand, or even use mops and pre-rinse your car before you go into the machine. Like anything else, prices vary, but basic washes cost from $3 to $10 and usually end up somewhere in the middle, with one glaring exception.

Mike's Express Carwash is a company in Indiana that sells automated car washes for $18, the going rate for the "Works" wash with "Tire Shine."

You read right. There's no hand drying, nothing done to the interior at all. They just roll your car through what might feel like any other automatic carwash. You stay in your car while it happens.

It's a good carwash, but is it the best? I don't know. Is it worth the money? No clue. Are they the busiest, fastest-growing carwash in the country? You bet.

Between radio, TV, billboards, and locations in every part of town and all around the state of Indiana, they're ubiquitous. I've seen $2 coupons print out on the back of a grocery receipt towards a Mike's Express Carwash at my local Kroger.

I'm almost certain that the owners of this company make millions of dollars (despite their recent split into "Mike's Carwash" and "Crew Carwash") and it's a good thing they took the advice of business consultants and learned the lessons other big businesses had instead of asking another carwash owner.

If they had listened to another carwash owner, they might have received some advice that is good, but not great. They might have heard about which carwash machines deliver the best carwash, or which ones do it the quickest, or maybe which ones have the lowest maintenance cost and are the easiest for staff to operate.

They might have been lucky enough to get some good advice about location and signage- two of the biggest drivers of business for most carwashes.

You don't perform thousands or even tens of thousands of carwashes per day at dozens of locations, each costing I would estimate around $2 million to build, by following advice from single-location owner-operators who serve only hundreds of customers monthly. If you listen to them, you'd probably get some really bad advice like, "If you just do the best wash you can, people will come back and tell their friends and you'll have a great carwash business."

By Mike's Express standards, following this line of thinking would result in a colossal failure.

That doesn't mean they don't offer a great carwash. They certainly don't strive to offer a mediocre one. Their customer service is amazing, but they have a lot of customers to serve and that's the key.

For most carwash owners, spending money on marketing is tough to do. They don't get a huge return, so they trickle their marketing efforts out slowly attempting to gain a customer whom they can turn into a repeat client and see a return...then they trickle out some more. Most of their marketing says two things:

1. Their location.

2. That they offer a great carwash.

Hopefully they focused on the hyper-local area so that location of the recipients of the message mattered a *lot*. The second part of the message is meaningless. It would be the same as a home inspector saying, "I do a good inspection." Of course they're going to say they have a good carwash.

Mike's does things differently. It's almost like there are people running the company who not only know how to wash a car, but also know how to run a business!

The message is simple: Mike's is the best carwash *because:*

- 1,000,0000 BTU water heaters. It doesn't matter whether you're the first car or the last car of the day or anywhere in between, you're going to get hot water.

- More blowers than any other carwash- and at higher power too! Your car will be dry!

- Buy "The Book"- Get six washes for the price of five and you can use them at any of their locations.

Then you show up and find a consistently sized, brick building, complete with all the vacuums and ancillary services you're looking for. Oh, and every associate is wearing a uniform with a tie. A tie at a carwash!

The guy down the street may offer a better carwash, but I will never know.

If you think home inspection is different than literally every other business in the world, then you need to just accept your place as a low-volume provider of service at market rates.

Home inspection is no different than other businesses- it's just incredibly fragmented and full of technicians, many of whom would be happy to work for someone else if they could actually be guaranteed a salary and benefits.

By following the standard SOP and not offering anything substantially different from your competition, you become inexpensive Vodka- served from the well of the bar to people that don't realize or don't have the means to understand that life is too short for bottom shelf liquor.

Chapter 8
Liability and Lies

Wool carpet in a solid color doesn't seem on its face to be a big deal. Frankly, I'm not a big fan. Give me hardwoods, slate, travertine, or even a really good carpet and I'm happy, but in the McMansions of Carmel, Indiana there are quite a few $2 million + houses that have wool carpeting. Expensive wool carpeting.

On one of those minor detours in my life between the last time I was fired by my parents and before I took over the home warranty company, I started a little property services business. Eventually I figured out that the most money to be made was in big contracts with management companies, which ultimately led to my being able to sell that company less than a year after starting it for pretty decent money at the time. But before I figured that out I went for the home runs in the form of McMansions.

I left fliers, made phone calls, offered everything from cleaning gutters to changing light bulbs and doing general maintenance to housekeeping services. Since most people don't trust their home maintenance needs to an eighteen-year-old who looks not a day over fifteen, I picked up a bunch of housekeeping clients.

What a pain in the butt.

I was still in high school, so I would assemble my staff in the mornings, I had around ten people within two months of starting the service, and I would assign them their jobs, and then I would check on them in-between classes.

There was one house I'll never forget. Probably a $1.7 million house at the time in 1999. It was around 12,000 square feet, half a dozen kids lived there, and the client was extremely particular about how things were cleaned. She would watch the team of three I'd send over there every Wednesday, two of whom couldn't speak English well.

It made them nervous.

Especially nervous was the newcomer to the group, his name escapes me. He was cleaning an upstairs bathroom, and it was right off this sizeable "bridge" between the master bedroom and the other bedrooms spanning the dramatic two plus story entryway.

He was using a bleach-based cleaner in the bathroom and he was being watched. He was looking away as he put the bottle down into his bucket, and he missed. The bottle hit the carpeting, the brownish-orange designer *wool* carpeting. At first it appeared just wet apparently. Over a period of about an hour it got lighter, and lighter, and then white as the perfect ring the size of the bottom of the bottle now showed brightly on what I thought was an otherwise ugly carpet.

I carried two cell phones in high school. One was forwarded from my office line so I never missed a call, the other for employees (and friends/family I suppose) to call me on. They both vibrated in my pocket, I excused myself from class to go to the bathroom (a.k.a. my "office"), and I took the call from the office line first.

It was the high-maintenance, pain in the butt homeowner.

She was bouncing off the walls, furious. I calmed her down, let her know it's just carpet, no big deal, we'll take care of it.

"But it's specialty carpet!"

I didn't argue with her, I just told her to get an estimate to fix it and get me a copy so I can look at it. I spoke to my employees, found out what happened, and the bottom line was this: *I was responsible.*

I was new to the business. I didn't want a big claim on my general liability insurance, but this shouldn't be a big deal. A couple hundred bucks, maybe?

Try $4,600.00.

$4,600.00 for some stupid wool carpet in what can't be a 200 square foot area, and of course no way they could patch it in.

You can do a lot with $4,600.00. You can replace both a furnace and an air conditioner. You can put a new roof on most houses. You can fix a major structural issue. You can mitigate the home for radon, treat it for termites, and have money to spare for a vacation.

$4,600.00 was a lot of money to an eighteen-year-old running his first business. I had payroll to meet, a mortgage to pay, and an addiction to fast cars to pursue. As painful as it was, I committed to take care of the issue.

Ultimately I found a company that specializes in coloring high-end carpeting, and the issue was resolved for less than $1,000. Had I not answered the client's phone calls, had I not committed to *solving the problem*, the client may not have accepted the repair.

I owe that to my parents and how they ran the business I grew up in. The had white Ford Rangers with blue logos, uniformed inspectors, letterhead and business cards, and computer-generated reports before anybody else in the business even had a computer. They answered the call before the third ring every time, and no they were not afraid to solve a problem even if it meant writing a check.

I'm not even positive when they started in the business that Errors and Omissions insurance for inspectors was available. I know it was uncommon. Very early on they did thousands of inspections each year when most of their competition did less than a hundred, and every once in a while there was a complaint. Less often, the complaint turned into a threat of legal action. Seldom, those threats turned into reality and what you've heard from other inspectors about that limitation of liability in the inspection agreement not necessarily holding up in court is absolutely true. It does sometimes, but not all the time.

The rule for us was simple: you don't go to court if you're in the wrong. Period.

So while other kids my age were enjoying being "kids", I was dressing professionally, printing up business cards, printing out professional invoices, and answering the phone every time it rang.

If this homeowner had been dealing with anyone else twice my age, they would have likely not accepted the repair. Liability has little to do with standards of practice or with contracts. These things are important, but the real test in the client's mind is how comfortable they feel throughout the process (your level of professionalism) and your response to their complaints.

Let's look at the various ways you can look professional, versus the less professional opposite:

Professional- The client calls to book an inspection, gets a professional phone answering staff member who takes their information, gets them scheduled, and then sends them a confirmation e-mail along with the inspection agreement and a detailed written proposal as to what the inspection includes. The phone is answered, "Thank you for calling Professional Home Inspections, this is Nicole, how may I help you?"

Unprofessional- Client calls and gets the inspector himself who answers the phone, or maybe a voice-mail that even says which cell phone service he uses and gets a call back. The inspector proceeds to take the order with background noise clearly indicating he is not in an office. There is no e-mail follow-up, and the person who answered the phone is the same person who shows up to do the inspection. The phone is answered, "Jim's Home Inspection Service".

The first company exudes confidence and professionalism. The client now has the name of not only the inspector, but also someone who works in the office at this professional organization they'd never heard of before they were referred by their real estate agent or found them on the Web. They feel good and know that if they have a question or an issue that they can call the business phone number any time, talk to a person, and get their issues resolved.

The second company, in this case "Jim" (he's the entire "company" in the client's mind, and it's never a good idea to have a word like "company" in quotation marks), has destroyed any possibility that he will ever be a true professional in the client's mind. The best he can hope for is a personal relationship and level of trust that he might be able to create once on-site, but that's about it.

This is where liability starts. After the inspection, after the closing, after the move-in, and after something doesn't work correctly, people have a tendency to want to get things fixed. If they have an air conditioning issue and they call a company with a big advertisement in the yellow pages, they're going to get a professional response. When that contractor then shows up in a big painted truck in a uniform with a professional bid for replacing the air conditioner for some ridiculously large sum of money, you're already behind the eight ball. When that company says (erroneously) that "Your inspector should have told you this thing needed to be replaced"...The client believes him!

If you were just as professional, showed up in a truck with your logo on it, had an office staff or a call center that made you look professional before you even showed up, you would be on a level playing field.

It doesn't matter what type of contractor we're talking about. It could be a plumber, a termite treatment company, a structural contractor, or a mold remediation firm- it doesn't matter. When people experience a problem, they don't automatically call an attorney and sue their home inspector. They have to have a reason to, and they have to go through a few stages to get there:

1. First Impression- was the inspector just an *inspector* with a truck, or was this a professional home inspection company with the resources to handle my issues?

2. Problem Found, Now What? – What do I do when there's a problem? Can I call the inspection company and get an immediate answer to my concern or will I just get the inspector's cell phone voice-mail? Will he even return my call in time for this problem to be resolved before it causes more problems in my life?

3. Where's the process? – When I called the contractor, they told me I should definitely go after the inspector for this. That if *they* had missed [fill in defect here] they would take care of it. So is there a process for handling this, or do I just get it taken care of. and deal with it later as the contractor suggests?

4. Demand- A request has been made to solve the client's problem. Whether it is a real problem or not has already been determined in their mind through stages 1, 2, & 3.

5. Resolution- The issue has either been resolved in the client's mind or it hasn't. If it hasn't, they continue to be active in seeking resolution.

There are a few frivolous exceptions to any of this, but short of the rare individual who is actually out to get you, acknowledgement of these stages and building systems to avert complaints every step of the way is a sure-fire way to reduce liability.

None of this relieves the need to have a good, solid contract or to be well versed in the minimum Standards of Practice, but the number one way to reduce liability is to be "more than just an inspector," be a *company*. A proven second way to reduce that same liability would be to offer 90-Day Warranties. The client confidence level in the inspector both when choosing a provider as well as when there is an issue later goes up tremendously.

Let me give you an example outside of the inspection business. Let's say you bought a car from a small car lot, the kind that doesn't have a brand affiliation like Penske or Tom Wood or Germain or whoever is the big car dealer in your area with brand affiliations and multiple dealerships. You purchased from the kind of car lot that doesn't have an indoor showroom and does not sell new cars.

They had the car you wanted; it's a used Ford Mustang for this example. You test drive the car, you buy it cash, and you take it home.

The next day the engine seizes.

What do you do?

I think most people might call the dealer, tell them about the issue, and see what they're willing to do about it.

What if they don't answer the phone?

What if they tell you that you bought the car "As-Is," no warranty?

What do you do next?

A few Google searches, maybe a call to an attorney or two, and about 24 hours of completely stressing out later, you'll come across your state's "Lemon Law," that usually says something to the effect that if you buy a total piece of garbage and it falls apart within seven days, the dealer either has to fix it or buy it back.

Now that you know the law exists, you confront the dealer about it, and they say, "Oh, we'll fix it."

You drop off the car and wait. Days pass. A week passes. No word.

It's clear that the dealer doesn't have the backing to deal with the issue, so they're likely shopping some hole in the wall auto shops trying to find someone to fix this issue on the cheap, which doesn't mean they're fixing it "well." This is of course nothing more than a theory on your part, but it's building up in the form of stomach acid until you finally call them and ask for your money back.

"We're fixing it, be patient."

Eventually you sue them for the sticker price of the car, and they don't show up in court. Then you pay your attorney (again) for a "proceedings supplemental" to actually collect on your default judgment, which only goes so far because you can't squeeze juice out of a turnip.

What if this whole issue was nothing but a simple fix, and there was legitimately a backup of service at the auto repair shop they took it to? What if they chose a mechanic who was known to be the best in the business at working on that year, make and model of car, and they genuinely wanted to get it fixed right for you?

None of that mattered.

They lost your confidence the minute the salesperson was also the finance guy and was also the guy to clean out the car and also the guy to handle your call when you had a complaint and you assume he was also the guy who bought the car at an auction in the first place.

Zero structure + Zero staff= Zero consumer confidence.

This is how many clients are made to feel almost immediately when they order a home inspection at most home inspection companies. Think about it.

Now let's take the same example from above, except you bought a used car at the largest dealership in town. Same thing happened. You brought it home and the engine seized. You call the dealership, explain the situation, they put you in contact with a service manager.

He has you bring the car in, they want to check it out and see what they can do.

They find the minor issue that appears to you like it is seizing, fix it, you pick up the car, and everything is fine.

Does it cost them some money to resolve these sorts of issues? Yes. Do they invest a lot of money in staff and resources to be able to handle complaints in this manner? You betcha. Do they have a better reputation and higher confidence from consumers in their products and have more repeat business? Oh yes. Do they charge more for their used cars than the tiny car lots out there and make bigger profits? Absolutely!

As a home inspection company owner, you have to make the decision as to whether you want to look like a greasy, low end used car dealer or a pristine, world-class, high end dealership.

How do you do that?

Simple. If you have more than three inspectors, hire someone to work as your office manager and answer the phones. If you have less than three inspectors, hire a call center. The two best are The Inspector Services Group and America's Call Center.

The other thing you need to do is have scripts. How you answer the phone every time it rings. "Jim's Home Inspection" is not a proper call answering script, and if you think I'm being harsh just go seek advice from counsel on your future bankruptcy now.

Try something more like, "Thank you for calling Security Home Inspections, this is Nathan, how may I help you?" I've only repeated those words tens of thousands of times. I could walk into that office right now and I would almost automatically reach for the phone when it rang and if I didn't stop myself I'd end up saying that to the person on the other line.

The final thing to do is to leave your ego at the door. If you're still in the field inspecting, and that's a good use of your time, when you're on site you are *not* the owner, the president of the company, or any other such nonsense. You are the inspector.

Print up business cards that say it. Wear a uniform. Install logos on your truck. Be a humble servant to your clients on inspections the way you want every inspector that ever works for you or carries on the business after you to do.

Then establish processes for dealing with complaints, a hierarchy to make sure clients have confidence in the process, and a policy that issues are tended to quickly, resolved efficiently, and dealt with before they cause the biggest liability of all, the one that happens a thousand times as often as an inspector going to court, losing future clients and referrals.

Chapter 9
The USP

Domino's Pizza, in 2011-2012, came out with an ad campaign they ran nationally that I like to call "Our Pizza Sucks!...But We're Fixing It." It was an interesting concept, and the results seem to indicate it worked. They would put people in a room, hand them a slice of Domino's pizza, and then show their negative reactions. Next they showed their pizza chefs fixing the problem, delivering the new and improved pizza to a participant in the study's front door, and the positive response to the new flavors.

The ads were brilliantly done, zooming in and focusing on the herbs and spices they put on the crust and boasting about improvements they had made to toppings. The first pizza I bought after I saw these ads was from Domino's.

Maybe you like the pizza, maybe you don't, but Domino's has some of the best marketing people in the world working at their corporate headquarters. In one of the most competitive foodservice industry sectors, Domino's skyrocketed past almost everybody to become the #2 pizza delivery company in the world.

They were able to do this for two main reasons; 1. They had a solid business plan. 2. They were the only pizza delivery company to differentiate themselves.

Domino's figured it out in 1973. They made themselves stand out in the marketplace by offering a guarantee that, "if you don't get your pizza in 30 minutes or less, it's free!"

This was revolutionary, and it scared the heck out of their competitors. In boardrooms and offices of the other pizza brands you could hear the shouts of executives losing market share, making excuses for not being able to offer the same guarantee.

"But what if we have to give a pizza away for free?"

"What if we get too many orders?"

Domino's did give away some free pizzas, but they sold more pizzas than everybody else, so who cares if they had to give away a free one here or there? It didn't add up to much.

They didn't have any problems keeping up with the demand or offering the guarantee in multiple countries. However, eventually there were some accidents involving Domino's delivery drivers and public perception of the guarantee had turned from gleeful to skeptical that drivers might be pushed to drive less than safely. The number of accidents they had weren't any worse than other pizza brands, it was nothing more than a perception issue and they were becoming a target for lawsuits as a result. *That wasn't until 1993 that they temporarily halted the guarantee-* and then in 2007 they brought the guarantee back in a slightly different form, because as it turns out differentiating yourself from the competition is a pretty darn profitable thing to do.

What do others in the pizza business do? They say they have good pizza, and then they try to be price competitive. That's it.

At least when it comes to food there are discernable differences in flavor. Some people prefer Pizza Hut or Papa John's for the taste, but if you asked the average consumer why they chose any particular pizza over another, you'd probably find that they weren't loyal to any particular brand. But in the late 80's and early 90's, during the period of Domino's largest growth, the answer was really simple: "Domino's delivers fast."

The *"delivered in 30 minutes or it's free"* campaign was what is known as a Unique Selling Proposition or a "USP." The term was invented by Rosser Reeves of Ted Bates & Company in the 1940's, and it was first introduced as a theory of why advertising campaigns of the time were successful in getting consumers to switch from one brand to another.

In order for a benefit to be a *Unique Selling Proposition* it must be one that others in the same business don't or can't offer. It must have the power to move the masses to your product or service, and it must say to the potential buyer of your products or services that "if you buy this product or service, you'll get this benefit".

It's sometimes referred to by the unenlightened as a "gimmick." I don't care what they call it, I call it profitable.

If you're in a service business like home inspection, you need to have offerings that make you *unique*. If you don't, every dollar you spend on Web development, Google ads, or printing of fliers and business cards is wasted. You're just another home inspector who wants business.

In the early days of Security Home Inspections, it wasn't hard to be unique. Most inspection companies didn't have an office that answered the phone and delivered reports and visited every real estate office in town regularly. Showing up and answering the phone and being a "real" business were enough to leave the competition in the dust.

As time passed, more inspectors were catching on to the importance of looking professional, so Security Home Inspections did some things that few inspectors had the resources to do. My dad spent the money and time he needed to in order to get a plumbing license, and my mother got her pest control operator's license. She was one of the only women in the classes, and the only person in the room who had no intention of offering treatment for termites and other wood destroying organisms at all- and likewise my dad was the only one in the room that didn't even own a plumber's torch.

It may have been expensive and painful at the time, but Security Home Inspections became the company that you could make *one call* to and get all of your home inspection needs done. They could now offer inspections, wood destroying pest reports, well and septic inspections, and water testing.

Real estate agents responded well to this concept. They didn't have to hand a client five or six different companies to call and get these different inspections arranged and *hope* their clients got all of these tests completed before the inspection response period expired. This was a huge benefit to both the buying and listing side. Security Home Inspections could also offer these tests for less than if you hired three or four different parties because they were already there, so the home buyers saw an immediate benefit in a reduction of cost in purchasing a home. Profits went up too.

Time passed and once again innovation was needed in order to stay ahead of the pack, and in 2001 Security Home Inspections became our first 90-Day Warranty client.

The pitch was simple, and once again their profit margins and market share went up. "With every full inspection we perform, you get a 90-Day Warranty so that even if something like your dishwasher is working perfectly fine at the time of your inspection, if you move in and it has a problem, you can call the warranty company and get it fixed."

This was their best USP to date, because it scared the heck out of their competition and made them look terrible at the same time. Prospective clients would call around to the three companies their agents referred them to, and after they called Security Home Inspections they would ask the next company not about their *price*, but rather if they offered a warranty with their home inspections.

Some inspectors were smart and just said "No." They still didn't book the inspection, but at least they didn't do what some others did and start lecturing the client about what an inspection is and that warranties aren't a part of their standards, etc.

After getting that lecture, more than one inspection company was actually removed from agents' referral lists because the clients didn't like being talked down to.

After several years, others in the marketplace started offering 90-Day Warranties, but still less than 10% of inspectors. The 90-Day Warranty remains today a USP that makes you different than most all of your competitors, and when implemented properly it renders any sales pitch a competitor might have useless. I'm fairly decent with words, and I can't figure out how to convince someone that *not* having a warranty is better than having one. The possibility to combat products like SewerGard, Moldsafe, and RecallChek as your competition is even slimmer.

The 90-Day Warranty is not the only way to make your company unique, there are endless possibilities. There are offerings from vendors like myself like RecallChek of course, discounts on alarm monitoring systems, Termite Protection Plans, SewerGard, MoldSafe, and then there are things you can put in place yourself. Some inspectors give each client a book on how to operate their home- some of these publications are original, some are purchased from third parties like The Ultimate Home Book from The Inspector Services Group. Some inspection companies offer free re-inspections (also referred to as "repair inspections"). Some offer them for a small fee and that's perfectly fine as well.

At Security Home Inspections, we always charged for our re-inspections but many of our competitors didn't offer them at all. It was great to hear the excuses... "I don't do re-inspections, I do inspections. If you want me to re-inspect a home, I'll do it for the full inspection fee because I don't know what else might have changed in the home."

When I was answering the phone for Security Home Inspections, on more than one occasion I had a buyer ask me if I would match the price of a particular competitor who I knew didn't offer re-inspections. *Every single time* I not only booked the order but did so at our full fee. All I had to do was tell the client the following:

"Ah, yes, [inspection company name], I'm somewhat familiar with them. They're a small operation I think on the west side, pretty new I believe. We don't match prices with anyone. Most companies know we're the market leader and tend to come in right below our pricing for that reason. One thing you might want to consider is that after we do the inspection and you have the seller make corrections, we offer to re-inspect those items and make sure they were repaired properly before you close on the house, and the fee for that is only $95- it's something I would recommend you consider doing. Any inspector confident in his abilities in inspecting your home should also be familiar with repair standards and all of our inspectors are familiar with those standards. If [inspection company name] doesn't offer re-inspections you should call them to find out why. I personally don't see why someone familiar with home systems wouldn't be capable of offering this service for you."

I let that other company do the rest of the selling for me.

Other Unique Selling Propositions used to include things like computer-generated reports and color digital photographs, but those are pretty standard now. By "standard" I mean to say "required."

I know of an inspector in Texas that after you get an inspection and move in, you get your lawn mowed for free.

Sound crazy? I won't name names but they're doing pretty darn well.

Some inspectors offer free pool and irrigation system inspections, which has the dual benefit of giving them the ability to increase their base inspection fees and the ability to target higher end homes (and agents). *Some inspectors don't like doing things for free, but if your base rate increases and your volume does as well- it's not really "free."*

Some inspectors (around 10% of them) offer RecallChek and check for recalls on every home they inspect, plus check for recalls every month for their clients for as long as they own their home. Nearly all of these inspectors charge more than their competition every day, and about a quarter of those inspectors pay nothing for this service.

Those same inspectors offer free e-mail newsletters from the agents to their clients.

Maybe none of these differentiators are for you or for your business and that's fine. Maybe you're going to be the inspector who revolutionizes the business for the next generation of inspectors.

Just don't go *backwards*.

Backwards takes us to one place and that's irrelevance sprinkled with poverty. When my parents did their first inspections, in the infancy of the industry, the inspection fees were in the $90 range, inspections took 45 minutes, and they were garbage. By today's standards, the inspections of thirty years ago would be seen as far from adequate. Today, average fees at the same company top $500, and nationally run around $300. *Imagine 30 years from today when most inspectors are checking for recalls, offering guarantees, and utilizing advanced tools in their inspection process like infrared cameras...we'll be talking about how "inadequate" inspections in 2012 were!*

When inspection companies come up with a new offering, they should be applauded. We should all hope that it takes hold, and adds to all of our bottom lines. Even the mediocre inspector with less business savvy than the five year old running your neighborhood lemonade stand owes the innovators of the early years for being competitive and taking the electrical panel cover off, buying a ladder and using it to get on the roof, and creating software in Access or FileMaker or buying it from Carl Fowler at 3-D. If they had not done these things, if they had been influenced at all at the time by those who called their trucks with ladders and computerized reports "gimmicks," then we would still be doing incomplete, inadequate, and cheap 45-minute home inspections.

There's a chapter in my second book, Change|Up, entitled "Your Fees are Not What you are Worth." If I could get every business owner to read it their world would change for the better-inspectors especially.

Chapter 10
The Mike Crow Effect

Carleton H. Sheets reigned supreme in late night infomercials for two decades. It's estimated that the total cost for airtime ran the company that promoted him around $280 million. That's a lot of airtime, and if you don't know who Carleton Sheets is and you work in this business, you need to learn a little bit about this real estate industry we work in.

His system was called *No Money Down*, and it was a guide to investing in real estate. There were books, audio books, CD's, and, of course, you could pay to attend one of Carleton's presentations as well.

Today, the world of real estate investing info-marketers is in shambles.

We all saw the infomercials, and many of us laughed at them. It must be "too good to be true." It's not believable.

We see on the screen examples of not-so-well-spoken individuals who are "students" of Carleton sitting next to their pool in front of their yacht and talking about how easy it is to make millions in real estate if we just follow Carleton's system.

Critics of Sheets and the half a billion dollars in sales he generated say that the method of selling the system was targeted at the naïve. This may be so, but that doesn't mean his system didn't have validity. In fact, there was a lot of sound advice he gave his "students."

How do I know?

Because I listened to every single audiotape he recorded his books and systems onto.

It wasn't by choice; this was happening between the ages of nine and twelve that I had to put up with it because back in those days there wasn't a separate entertainment system in the back of every mom-mobile like there is now. Every tape of Carleton's monotone voice, the Mr. Rogers of real estate, was played in my mother's van for three years straight.

My parents weren't naïve. They were very smart and they knew that Carleton Sheets was being listened to by 100's of thousands of real estate investors (a.k.a. "potential clients"), and they wanted to know more about their clients than anyone else. That way they could speak intelligently on investment issues when they were brought up by agents and clients alike. Maybe Sheets wasn't the only source, but he was a good starting point.

They picked up some great advice on real estate investing. They went on to pick up a few more resources, spoke to their bankers and attorneys, and started buying properties.

There were undoubtedly a large majority of Carleton Sheets students who had no idea what they were doing, or didn't follow the system, or both, that got into trouble making bad investments or didn't even buy a single house.

On the other end of the spectrum, there were thousands of people like my parents who took his system, perfected it for their own uses, and went to town building wealth in real estate. If my parents ever decide to retire, they can do so to their choice of multiple properties they hold in sunny, sandy, beach and island locations. What suckers they are for spending almost $500 on the full "No Money Down" system!

By the time I graduated high school, I had already purchased two properties. One was the house in which I lived and had significant equity in, the other was a condo I had rented out and was cash-flowing quite nicely. Both had been purchased without any involvement from my parents, I'm not sure they would have been very supportive of my plans if I had ever told them, but I had the knowledge, much of which had come from those Carleton Sheets tapes.

That's why it makes no sense that to this day I am the most skeptical person I know. I still watch infomercials and laugh. I still see "coaches" and "consultants" as a waste of time and money.

It's why I understand completely why some of the home inspectors who see Mike Crow do one of his presentations will later say, "He's full of it. Why would I pay him for his advice?" I also understand why some inspectors won't listen to him at all.

It took me a good long conversation with myself before I finally decided to put this chapter in the book. There's a certain *risk* to telling anyone what he or she ought to hear. It's kind of like seeing someone (much bigger and angrier than you) drinking in a bar and suggesting that they stop before drink number eleven and ask them for the keys to the car you saw them drive up in. It's the right thing to do. I've done it on multiple occasions, but sometimes they take a swing at you or get even angrier.

There's nothing you can do for them.

You, on the other hand, have made it pretty far through a pretty intense book that not a lot of stubborn, petty, unsuccessful inspectors are going to like so I have confidence that you can handle this statement:

Try Mike Crow's system, spend a few hundred bucks, and if it's not for you stop.

It's not for everybody. There were hundreds of thousands of people who completely failed on Carleton Sheets' systems, but thousands of others who thrived.

I think the numbers are at least a little better when it comes to Mike Crow's members of his "Millionaire Inspector Community." I *know* they are- because we track those numbers. *I think the name of his group is as cheesy as you might-* and so do many of his members by the way. It's all very intentionally outrageous.

Here's another statement I think you can probably handle:

Sixteen of the top 25 Inspector Services Group clients are members of Mike Crow's organization, and those companies on average do more than *15 times* as many inspections as the average inspector in the U.S. and Canada.

Several of the other companies in that top 25 list have been a member of Mike's organization at one time or another. Some of them like his stuff and just didn't need him anymore...they had "graduated" in their minds. Others didn't like the advice, or left for other reasons. Push comes to shove, all of them would likely say the return on investment was good.

It's hard to believe that the statistical domination these companies all have in common over their competition is a coincidence.

You may think it's all bull, and that's okay. Just because you don't subscribe to Mike Crow's, or anyone else's stuff for that matter doesn't make you unsuccessful or unintelligent. You might even feel "stupid" for needing help growing your business. You would probably feel like a fool for ordering Carleton Sheets' system in the late 80's or early 90's, but it *might* have been the best thing that ever happened to you. It might have inspired you to do something, even if you didn't take the specific advice and implement it.

That's the way it works with Mike's stuff as well, but if his style isn't your cup of tea, find something that is. Get involved in a mastermind group, bring in a consultant, or even get someone from outside the profession to work with you on a growth strategy. Call another coach like Ken Compton or get to an inspection seminar and attend some of the business courses. None of this can hurt.

I once spent $4,000 to go to one seminar. I also spent over $25,000 for three days of consulting at one point.

Laugh if you want to.

I would estimate my returns from those two expenditures, totaling less than $30,000, to be a number I'm not even comfortable publishing. I've also sought the advice of Mike Crow on many occasions, and not once was I disappointed with the results. Sometimes I ignore his advice, but that doesn't mean I don't take it under consideration.

No, I won't tell you what Mike Crow's advice is. Not because I'm bound by any sort of confidentiality, it's more a matter of the information needing to be presented in a certain way in order for it to be effective. In other words, I could tell you a few things and you could use the advice in a way that doesn't help you and may even hurt you.

I will tell you this: 80% of what Mike says is common sense stuff that everyone should be doing but we often forget and need that motivation to keep up on the basics. The other 20% is cutting edge stuff to keep you ahead of the competition. Some of it works great, some of it is so-so. You won't know until you implement it and every market is a little different.

A few hundred dollars buys you the full experience for a couple of months, take from it what you want to. He'll send you a package and invite you to some conference calls. I personally know over a hundred inspectors who have seen double and even triple digit growth in their volume *and* revenue with Mike. Probably half of them needed the information and the other half already knew most of it but couldn't put together an organized plan of attack without some guidance.

I've also seen the same from clients who implement our products and services, I've seen it from franchisees of HouseMaster, Pillar to Post, HomeTeam, WIN, and others as well.

It's really about having a mindset that allows you to take advantage of the systems and experiences of others. Give Mike Doerr in my office twenty minutes of your time and see what he can do for your Website. If you're a franchisee, grab every resource you can from corporate.

If you would rather take on the world yourself and be a one-man army, good for you. I used to be that guy, and I was proud of what I did every day regardless of the results. Just be prepared to make every mistake everyone else has made getting to where they are.

You may never get where you want to be, but at least you did it your way!

Chapter 11
Agent Haters

If it weren't for my grandfather's love of the great American steak, I would not be here today.

It may seem like a strange statement, but *Don Thornberry's Steak Place* was a legendary restaurant in Carmel, Indiana. To this day I still run into people who ate there almost weekly and got personal visits at their table from Don.

After running the most profitable *Bonanza* restaurant in the country, my grandfather opened an independent steak house right on the main road running through Carmel. It was a noticeable feature in the landscape, and as a good supporter of the community, he sponsored things like the Carmel High School yearbook, even though his oldest son and very decent grill worker, Phil (my father), went to a private high school in Indianapolis.

I'm not sure if it was the location of the restaurant or one of the advertisements that drove a girl named Patty to go and apply, but she did, and that steak house is where she met Phil, and even though they were only in high school at the time, they eventually married and had me at a relatively young age.

I eat steak almost every day religiously.

Probably not the best choice for my body or longevity, but everything good that ever happened to me started with a steak as far as I'm concerned.

Including an incredible real estate career for Don.

My grandfather later became a real estate agent and worked with a couple of big firms, ultimately at two of the largest Re/Max franchises in the state.

The relationships he had made as a proprietor in the restaurant business and his incredible negotiation skills led him to eventually get a couple of enormous builder contracts. To this day he's got one of the highest all-time sales records in the entire industry. Out of the 1.5 million active real estate agents in the country today, you might find a handful who sell the volume of real estate he did each year, and he kept it up for decades.

I was lucky enough to be the eldest of the grandchildren by a long shot, and as such I probably had more time with Grandpa Don before he died than my brothers or cousins did, which I will be eternally grateful for.

He was a pilot, a boater, an entrepreneur many times over, and probably had the highest level of integrity of anyone I've ever met.

"Don't do anything you wouldn't want on the front page of the newspaper the next day," he would tell me.

When you sell as much real estate as he did, you have the pleasure of interacting with pretty much anybody selling homes in the area. Spending days with him over the summers, I would be in his home office as he was dealing with the latest issue standing between his seller or buyer and the closing of a deal. Most of the time, all parties were civil and easy to deal with. Occasionally, there were fireworks as one of the parties redefined "crazy."

Being there from the start of a transaction to the very end, witnessing tens of millions of dollars in transactions in a single summer season (with occasional breaks for a matinee and McDonald's), you begin to understand what agents truly deal with.

The ignorant views of some inspectors who seem to think that many agents in the profession would just as soon sweep a structural issue under the rug and let their clients deal with the consequences later just aren't true.

Since those summers, between our one-year warranties, 90-Day Warranties, RecallChek reports, Radon Protection Plans, Termite Protection Plans, SewerGard, MoldSafe, InspectorLab, Home Inspection University, the Power User Conference, and other services we offer, I've been on some level involved in around $400 Billion in real estate transactions in every state and province/territory- more than any single inspector, mortgage broker, title company, or insurance agency throughout the U.S. and Canada- and throughout those transactions and that more than 15 years of experience I can tell you with absolute certainty that an insanely high percentage of real estate agents treat every single deal as if they were buying the house for themselves.

Those are the facts, *whether you want to accept them or not is up to you.*

Public opinion is on my side here as well. In a Gallup poll in 2011, when respondents were asked if the ethical standards of people in a number of different fields were very high, high, average, low, or very low, 70% of respondents gave real estate agents average or above. In fact, they ranked higher than attorneys. They were ranked higher than stockbrokers. They were ranked higher than insurance salesmen, senators, governors, labor union leaders, and business executives.

Let's do a little math here to assess the value of the opinion of an inspector in the category of "Agent Hater." One of those inspectors who chooses to take the path of most resistance on a daily basis and be at war with the agents who refer better than 80% (and likely over 90%) of the inspection business that happens throughout North America.

Let's say the inspector is average, which might be a generous assumption considering his disdain for the best referral source in the home inspection business, but let's say he does in fact book and complete 200 inspections annually.

Let's say 50% of those homes, once again being generous, had a significant structural issue, the kind agents supposedly don't want to hear anything about.

That's 100 inspections.

Let's now say that half of those, 50 inspections in total, had a buyer's agent present at them that actually approached the inspector in the way it gets told on forums and at chapter meetings, usually starting with, "You won't believe what this agent said to me..."

Fifty inspections.

Let's say they're in a market like Indianapolis with 20,000 transactions that happen every year. That comes out to ¼ of 1%.

If you made ¼ of 1% on a stock, would you get on the phone and start telling all your friends about it? Would you assume your stockbroker was a genius and invest your entire retirement fund with him and tell him to go to town?

Or maybe it's better to ask it this way, if you *lost* ¼ of 1% on a stock that your stockbroker had suggested, would you make sure everyone knew how bad he was and how no one should ever talk to him ever?

This phenomenon in the home inspection industry of small-time inspectors demonizing the entire real estate industry over their random, exceptional situations is unlike anything you'll find in any other industry.

What's more likely going on is that these inspectors who seem to run into a real estate agent who hates them everywhere they turn, probably didn't have the finesse they needed when they first got into the business. As a result, they had some bad experiences and have been fighting (losing) the war ever since.

It's sad really.

If this sounds like you, I am truly and sincerely sorry. I want to help you and I hope to accomplish this in two paragraphs.

In my experience, the bigger the inspection company, the less disdain and mistrust they have for real estate agents, which is good news for you. This means that the more transactions you do, the smaller the sampling of over-aggressive agents you might run into. That's hope for the future right there.

Regardless, let's say that agents truly do have it in for inspectors. *They are your referral source.* Put on a smile, play nice, and learn to get along with them. If that doesn't work, find an agent willing to let you shadow him for a week. After a week of living in their shoes, I promise you will have a better understanding of where they are coming from.

That is truly the key: *Understanding.*

It goes both ways. If you accept an education from an agent about what they deal with every day, they'll look forward to hearing the same from you. We're all on the same team, making sure the transaction is completed with accuracy and on fair terms for all parties.

If you are *truly* a good inspector, and you feel that any buyer in your marketplace would be well-served by having you as their home inspector, then stop being a hypocrite and do what it takes to represent more buyers. That means understanding the real estate business in its entirety, not just what you want to see in your little bubble.

If you have someone in your market that is the stereotypical "Agent Hater," take full advantage of that. *They are doing your marketing for you every time they open their mouths.* Some of them even have Websites telling one-sided stories of unethical agents. Agents in your area deserve to know who the "deal killers" are, and the pitch goes something like this;

"I'm a home inspector, but I'm also a part of your team and we're working for the same people with the same goal in mind. Not every home I inspect is perfect, in fact almost none of them are, but there's almost nothing that can't be fixed and I find it easier to approach issues both major and minor calmly and professionally. Unfortunately, there are some in my profession who see things differently and pretty much start the relationship with your client in an alarmist mode, at times even attempting to distance your client from their advisor in the transaction, you. I'm here to understand how I can do my job well while at the same time making your job easier, and I look forward to being a part of your team."

Make no mistake about it. Don Thornberry wanted the inspection company to find anything that they should. Give him a problem, he'll fix it. Like most agents, he will give you the opportunity to borrow his clients for a few hours if you have a solid reputation, but return them with undue anxiety and fear over a perfectly repairable issue, and you won't be hearing from any of his clients ever again.

A thorough inspection does not equate to an inspection that agents don't like, as much as some inspectors would like you to think is the case. An inspector with the personality and charm of sandpaper is what agents don't like, and if they don't like you that's why. Fix it.

Chapter 12
How to Install a Toilet

The coolest guy in the home inspection business is Jeff Donaldson. You may not know who I'm talking about, so let me tell you about Jeff. He is the owner of a multi-inspector firm in Charleston, South Carolina, and he's got a business that is kicking everybody's butt in his market.

Besides being a home inspector, he's also an Engineer, and he's got a program for inspectors that allow them to offer certain Engineering services. It's called "My Engineer On Call."

All that makes him successful and a good guy to know if you're a home inspector, but what makes him cool is this:

He's one of the few people in the world who handled nuclear weapons.

If we had been put in the position of shooting one into Russia, he would have potentially been the guy to push the button from the nuclear-powered submarine he worked on in the Navy, or at least he would have been standing pretty close to the guy who did.

That's pretty cool.

It's surprising how humble he is about this experience, like it's no big deal. He was a mile below the ocean's surface in a nuclear powered submarine filled with enough firepower to wipe out a good part of the earth's population if aimed at the right spot, and it's no big deal to him. *I may have exaggerated on the "mile below the surface" part, and Jeff would probably say the reactor was really a lot more interesting than the weapons, but for all of us non-engineer civilians the whole thing is like a movie.*

If I ever do anything half that cool, you will all know it. This might be the reason the U.S. Department of Defense entrusted Jeff with nuclear materials and not me.

Perhaps if this part of Jeff's biography were in the program for the 2011 ASHI Inspection World in Phoenix, he would have had more than the 50-75 inspectors he did have in the course he taught.

Instead of taking Jeff's course on marketing lessons he had learned in his business, the majority of inspectors headed down the hall to the larger room where they were teaching a course on proper toilet installation.

I actually don't know if it was a course on toilet installation. It may have been, but if it wasn't it may as well have been.

Inspectors in Jeff's course got quite a treat. He gave them twenty or more things that he does in his business that have given his business the boost that took him from one inspector to four or five in a mid-level market like Charleston. He's in the top ½% of inspection companies by volume nationwide and he wasn't there to sell anything, only to pass on his knowledge to others seeking it. He gets an expense paid trip to InspectionWorld, which is good enough for him. He likes to give back.

I went to watch for a few minutes, and I was pleasantly surprised when he touched on RecallChek, 90-Day Warranties, and even the ISG Call Center. Come to think of it, I still owe him a steak dinner.

He talked about all sorts of other things as well. Things that like RecallChek and 90-Day Warranties work and get him more referrals from real estate agents and past clients every day.

Going to seminars and conferences is important and technical courses are important. Courses that teach marketing and business practices are equally, if not more, important to most inspectors, so take a look at the courses and pick at least two business courses at every conference you go to. It's a sure-fire way to get out of the conference at least what you put into it in the way of airfare, hotel stays, admission fees, etc.

I'm proud of what ASHI has done over the last several years in the way of business courses. They've really stepped it up. Inspection World Phoenix was one of my favorite conferences of all time, and since then ASHI had a great show in Vegas.

Let me give you my top ten conferences in no particular order:

1. Power User Conference (Indy, Fall) – For Business Owners Only

2. The ISG/Home Inspection University Conference (Vegas, Spring)

3. Inspection World

4. Southeastern Conference

5. CREIA (California)

6. NAHI Annual Conference

7. Pro-ASHI (Pittsburgh)

8. CREIA

9. Great Lakes ASHI Chapter

10. FABI

If you go to any of these conferences seeking some advice on growing your business, you'll find it in the form of courses as well as a vendor hall full of the top vendors in the industry ready to demonstrate what they can do for your business.

If you don't belong to more than one of the groups listed above, join. Go to at least two conferences every year with different groups. It's what the most successful inspectors in the business do. I can tell you from being at more than fifty conferences a year that anyone in Florida would benefit from going to NAHI's conference even if they attend every FABI meeting. Inspectors in Pittsburgh who go to every Pro-ASHI meeting would gain incredible insight by attending a CREIA conference (most won't do that of course, but they should go to the Home Inspection University show in Vegas).

Many of the inspectors I work with belong to ASHI, NAHI, and InterNACHI- and why not? What is the real cost of getting the information other inspectors in your market are getting from their associations as well as your own? A small membership fee every year. That's it.

I get that InterNACHI is the biggest, ASHI is the oldest, NAHI has some incredible benefits, and some of the state organizations are more specific to local needs. I know some of these organizations take issue with some of the others, but I don't care and you shouldn't either. You need to do what's best for *YOUR* business. That means getting everything you can from every available resource, and getting your technical requirements out of the way quickly to make room for the business and marketing aspects of what some of these organizations provide.

After all, there's only so much to learn about toilet installation.

Just don't make the mistake of assuming that an Inspector Association is a marketing cooperative. Don't link to an association from your website, don't put the association logo in front of your own, and always put your business first. It's the responsible thing to do.

Chapter 13
Pricing Yourself out of the Market

The latest cycle of ratings from the American Customer Satisfaction Index resulted in a list of *The 15 Most Disliked Companies in America*. Amongst the fifteen, four of them were airlines.

United, Delta, U S Airways, and American Airlines all made the list.

If it had been a list of the 25 or 30 most disliked companies, every major carrier would have most likely made the list.

I knew they would be on there. Not because they want people to be unhappy, but because of the airline industry and the environment in which they operate.

If you have to ask why people hate the airlines, you must not fly much. Ask anyone who flies frequently, they'll rattle off a list of issues.

Small, uncomfortable seating, inefficient boarding methods, delays, not doing enough for their passengers when there are delays, dated planes without televisions and Wi-Fi, not enough direct flights, fees for baggage, fees for sitting in an exit row, minimal level of service, and the cost to fly is too high and inconsistent.

The only airline I *knew* wouldn't be on that list was Southwest. Why? Southwest is the only airline with a different business model. They book many of their flights on their own Website, they don't assign seats, you don't have to wait for first class to board before you do, and they don't charge for baggage.

Oh, and every Southwest plane is the same, a 737. That means their crews are all trained for every plane in the fleet, and delays due to staffing are incredibly infrequent. Plus their maintenance guys only have to work on one type of aircraft and they only have to stock parts for 737's.

There's a lot to be said for having something that makes your business unique, it can help you overcome incredible challenges like the primary reason the airlines end up at the top of the most hated list- pricing.

Airlines have taken fare models to the extreme with their availability-based pricing. Every time a seat is booked on an airplane, the price changes for all remaining available seats. Booking at the last minute is going to be incredibly expensive if there are only a couple of seats left.

Next time you're on a plane, ask the person next to you how much they paid. It could be half of what you paid or it could be double or triple. The airlines charge as much as they possibly can for every seat on an airplane and they're proud of it.

I believe that most inspectors charge too little. Not for what they're offering, but for what they should be offering. Add some benefits to your inspection, increase your fee, but don't go crazy.

I know of a couple of inspectors in different parts of the country who tried the "pricing on availability" model...and it hurt their business badly.

Even in a multi-inspector environment, managing such a pricing structure is messy. Even if you master the management of the pricing, you're still going to run into the problem of your inconsistent pricing turning off agents and clients alike.

As it turns out, agents like consistency. They *really* don't like it when they refer a client to your company and they get a price that is so far out of line with everyone else that it makes them look bad for strongly recommending you.

While these inspectors had a great concept when it came to implementing a progressive pricing structure and I applaud them for creativity, in practice it did nothing but lose them referral sources gradually throughout the busy season so badly that by the fall the availability pricing system had cost them huge amounts of money. Many times over what they made by charging a few home buyers basically whatever they were willing to spend during the busiest months.

It's not just the pricing method that can lose you customers. The pricing itself can be a problem.

I know quite a few inspectors who charged what I would call exorbitant fees for inspections at one point or another, and usually started doing so in a great market. Not just high prices, but incredibly high prices.

It worked for them for a month or two, maybe even a year...but the idea that they could do fewer inspections for massive profits turned out to be short-lived as once again the rule that agents don't appreciate looking bad took hold.

When all of your competition is at or below $500 for their base inspection fee in your area, and you're at $1500, at some point you're going to lose the business. It's that simple. There's only one exception to this I've ever seen work consistently and it is in a very high end area (homes predominantly over $2 million) and the inspector arrives with a whole team in a specialty vehicle more suited for military operations. They can inspect 10,000 square feet in an hour and a half. They also offer around 50+ value added services (some of which come from The Inspector Services Group).

Outside of that, all it takes is one dinner conversation between your client and a friend of his who spent 1/3rd of what your client did and conceivably ended up with the same results, and they are calling their agent to ask them why they had to pay so much.

The agent may love you, he may be your biggest fan, but he can only defend your price structure to so many clients before he has to figure out another way to do business and may not even call you to tell you why you're off the list.

Airlines can get away with this. There are only so many choices and they're all similarly priced to begin with- Inspectors not so much.

The best thing to do to maximize profitability is to figure out whether or not you're going to go multi-inspector or remain a single inspector firm. Then you can approach the pricing dilemma intelligently.

Let's start with single inspectors who have no intention of ever being a multi-inspector firm. Maybe you don't want to manage people, maybe your market isn't big enough to support multiple inspectors, whatever your reason I understand completely.

So let's figure out what hours you want to work, how many days you want to work, and how many inspections you can do comfortably in that time period.

Maybe it's two per day, five days per week for a total of ten inspections per week, with two weeks off each year, for a total of 500 inspections.

Now go pick up a rock, throw it thirty feet in any direction, and you will find someone who will at this juncture give you very bad advice. They're everywhere...people who believe they are giving you good advice by telling you to raise your prices. They'll point to an equation where a website or a book somewhere shows that reducing your price by 30% makes it so you have to sell 66% more product to make the same profit and that by simply raising your price by 10% you increase profitability by 25% or some other nonsense that's based on manufacturing a widget and then selling it out of a store that has ridiculously low overhead.

These people know nothing of the home inspection business. They really don't know that much about business at all. Parrots have the ability to repeat in the same way they do.

Let's actually come up with a solution to deliver you maximum profitability and consistent pay. The kind of business you'd like to have for your own sanity.

The key to raising prices is not doing it initially, but rather once you have volume. Raising your price $20 on 100 inspections is a total of $2,000. Raising your price $20 on 500 inspections is $10,000. Which one would you rather have?

Of course the answer is the larger of the two, so the key is having that volume of business to raise the rate on. That means inspections coming in at the rate you need to in order to make business come your way- profitably.

In other words, figure out your basis (cost of doing an inspection) and price your inspections above that but below the highest prices in the area in order to give your marketing message the best chance at success in acquiring new referral sources, also known as real estate agents.

Maybe you do 100 inspections this year, and maybe 200 next year. Don't make a substantial move in pricing. Keep building the number of inspections, and be patient.

Keep marketing, add to your services, make your company unique. Keep your referral sources happy and get your volume up toward 400 per year.

Now raise your price a bit, and make sure the business remains stable. Raise it a bit more, but keep in line with competitors to some extent. Add more services to increase your average ticket without raising fees, and tack on some value-adds as well to your base inspection.

Now go back out and market yourself with the higher fee schedule, and see if you can fill the rest of your schedule without too much difficulty.

If bringing on new clients to replace any lost referral sources proves either very difficult or impossible, you've hit a price point that your current marketing message cannot support. It's not a debatable point- it's absolute.

That doesn't mean your prices retreat. If you've managed to keep the original volume you built up and your referral sources remain loyal, you just need to change your offering.

Add some USP's. Do some sales meetings and educational sessions for agents. Hire a marketing representative to get your message in front of more agents. You can even do this on a part-time basis.

Eventually you're going to find the balance where you're making a very good profit on each inspection while also refraining from tying a pricing noose around your business and making it impossible to acquire new referral sources to replace those that leave the business or go elsewhere for whatever reason.

For those looking to become a multi-inspector firm, the pricing puzzle becomes a great deal more complicated. It's part of a much bigger topic as well: The Multi-Inspector Mindset.

Chapter 14
The Multi-Inspector Mindset

In the early 80's when Security Home Inspections was founded, there wasn't an Internet. There weren't inspector training schools like there are today.

Phil & Patty Thornberry had no idea what a home inspection company was supposed to look like, and there were few competitors. The one right down the street was Surette & Associates, owned by Dave Surette. He had multiple inspectors and ran the business out of a house that had been converted into an office. He had three sons who eventually got into the family business, and when the time was right he passed on the torch and went on to found RAL, the company that sources the lion's share of relocation inspections throughout the U.S.

Dave Surette had office staff answering the phone and did a pretty decent job of branding his business. I'm not sure how much Dave influenced the way my parents conducted their business in the early days, but it seems hardly coincidental that they did everything they needed to in order to get that first office...about a quarter mile away from Dave's and on the same street (Now a burger joint called "Bub's"). Dave and Phil would often see each other in the morning at the post office, with incoming mailboxes on the same wall.

Phil and Patty Thornberry took the brand name of Phil's electrical contracting business (Security Electric) and Patty's knowledge of the real estate transaction, and went to town building what would become one of the largest inspection companies ever. You can't do that without multiple inspectors to cover demand when you get ten, twenty, or even fifty plus orders per day.

It was common sense to them that the limiting factor to home inspection growth was capacity.

This is the defining characteristic of someone who has the multi-inspector mindset. They look at the business model and go into it wanting to serve as many clients as possible, being involved in as many real estate transactions as possible, and creating jobs through expansion.

Profit is certainly a consideration, but it's almost secondary.

For the inspector with the multi-inspector mindset, the goal of being the biggest and the best is much more exciting than making the most money off any single home inspection. It's the thrill of growth, getting more business, and being more competitive than anyone else in the market.

The single-inspector mindset is much more subdued- it focuses primarily on the inspection process itself. Some will even get to the point that hiring another inspector might be a good business decision, but they don't. They might be concerned that the next guy will be a liability or won't be as good as *they* are at inspecting. They may just not want to manage people, and that's a perfectly respectable position.

I'm the opposite. I want hundreds of employees, offices in every major city, and a brand that is recognizable coast to coast.

You could tell me that I would be happier, even perhaps wealthier, with a medium-sized company with a staff of less than twenty, but I wouldn't be interested. That sounds boring.

If you're the same way, you've got the multi-inspector mindset. If you don't, there's nothing wrong with you and no book will change who you are. Read the rest of this book five times and skip this chapter. Come back if something changes.

There's nothing more important than doing things your way, and being happy about it. Your way may include not having employees, and that's perfectly fine.

Now let's examine the structural changes you'll need to make in order to be successful as a multi-inspector firm.

If the name of your inspection company includes your first or last name or both, you need to seriously consider making a change. As a multi-inspector firm, you need to be able to schedule inspections with your staff. If your name is on the door, people are going to want you and they'll potentially feel cheated if they don't get you. It might be painful, but the longer you wait the more painful it is. You may be able to use the name you have but convert it to an acronym. For instance, if your company is called "P. Nathan Thornberry Home

Inspections," you could very easily transition to "PNT *Professional* Inspections," adding the potential for light commercial inspections as well.

Now that the name is determined, clients absolutely need to get the sense that when they call you they are dealing with an enterprise. If your cell phone is your company phone number, change it. If you personally answer every phone call, get a call center. Inspector Services Group offers one free for 60 days and cheap thereafter. There's really no excuse not to look professional these days in the home inspection business.

If you're going to build a big inspection business, it can't be based on your personality or personal ability to sell your service. You need to create a system for taking orders, and either place that in the hands of a call center or hire an office administrator to handle the calls. If the system doesn't work, fix it.

At any given time at Security Home Inspections, ten phone lines can light up and eight of those calls might be orders. Calling people back is not an option. The staff is in place; they're all perfectly qualified to take an order. Will they do it as well as Phil or Patty Thornberry the owners, himself or herself? Probably not, but the business is not Phil & Patty. It's Security Home Inspections.

Now comes the painful part for most inspectors.

Is your inspection process efficient and replicable?

From the process of inspecting itself, to filling out reports and delivering them, is the process something that could be learned by someone with basic home inspection training in a period of 90 days?

The immediate response you just had in your head is very telling. Maybe you thought to yourself, "Yes!" If that's the case, it should be smooth sailing. If the answer was either "No," "Not Really," or "Umm..." then we have a problem.

How many 1,500 square foot home inspections can you do in a day?

If it's two or three (preferably three), this is going to be easy for you.

If it's one, you have a problem. A serious problem.

If your goal were to be a single man operation, the answers to these questions wouldn't really matter much. If you're personally comfortable with what you do, great, but as soon as you start hiring staff and you have committed to keeping them busy, one inspection per day just doesn't cut it.

Your inspection needs to have plenty of comments ready to go, and it needs to come out of a system that's easy to use and scalable to any number of inspectors. You need to seek out someone in the inspection software industry who has experience in this- like Carl Fowler with 3-D or Dominic Maricic of Home Inspector Pro or John Kwasnik of Horizon. These three I have personal experience with specifically implementing multi-inspector firms.

Don't worry so much about the process until you get the report down, because a good, easy to use report can help you greatly in defining a process for your future inspectors.

Stay away from software that doesn't allow you to brand yourself exclusively. This is extremely important. You need to brand yourself. When you brand someone else, clients can very easily find a smaller competitor with the same system and think, "They're the same, only cheaper."

This is something you want to avoid.

Likewise, there are newsletter services out there, free websites, all sorts of resources that would be fine if only they focused on *YOUR* brand. If these types of resources come from an Association, they're probably better than nothing at all, but they're really harmful to your overall growth because of the opportunity to refer clients elsewhere.

This is just one area where it's worth mentioning that The Inspector Services Group really meets your need to brand yourself. Everything we do is branded with the inspector's logo and we ensure the inspector gets credit for everything (or the agent who referred him, whichever makes sense). Websites, newsletters, home maintenance books, everything we do is branded to you and we wouldn't have it any other way.

Which brings us back to the pricing models we covered in the last chapter. With a multi-inspector firm, pricing becomes an incredibly complicated labyrinth.

You really have to take into consideration so many factors that a simple equation to follow just doesn't exist. To some extent, you are limited by supply and demand and prevailing rates, but at the same time a well-branded multi-inspector firm can become a trailblazer when it comes to setting inspection standards and pricing as well.

Running a multi-inspector firm is much more about running a business than it is about home inspecting. If you decide to go down that path, it will be stressful at times, but incredibly rewarding.

Chapter 15
SOPs are so Twenty Years Ago

The various Standards of Practice that exist today from the major inspection organizations as well as the state licensing agencies are by and large good. There's nothing inherently wrong with having a minimum standard for an industry.

SOPs offer two specific benefits to home inspectors:

1. They make public a set of minimum standards, giving credibility to membership in an association or licensure.

2. They set parameters for inspections as general guidelines to prevent us having to "reinvent the wheel."

If we didn't have standards, both in ethical matters and in how we inspect, our industry would likely not have the credibility it does in the public eye. Some believe that the SOPs are liability protection and they are not. The only reason they serve to reduce our liability is that they give us minimum guidelines within which to operate, and prevent inspectors from doing lower-grade inspections that would not include the basics.

The exception to that would be if the standards are included or referenced in your inspection contract, at which point they become the definition of your scope of inspection. In that case, yes the SOPs serve as a limited layer of liability protection. I say "limited" because I've met a few judges and I've yet to meet one who takes the time to read the SOPs or acknowledges them in any meaningful way. The SOPs aren't inherently something a consumer is mindful of, and usually the contractor's opinion of the defect and whether it was "noticeable" gets asked. That's what the judge goes by much more than a standard you put forth that he's never heard of, is not going to read, and doesn't really care about because he's looking for *you* to show how you did not damage the other party. Was it "unavoidable" or outside of your control? Are you leaning on these standards as an excuse for negligence? I know, it's hardly fair, but it's reality.

The other reason I say SOPs provide very "limited" liability protection is because lawsuits and errors & omissions claims rarely come about as a result of an inspector *exceeding* the minimum standards and finding problems they would have otherwise missed or had no obligation to find in the first place. Claims and lawsuits are more likely the result of bad communication, frivolous/crazy clients out to cost someone money, the inspector not meeting the minimum standard in the first place, or rather, missing something he should have caught while performing an inspection up to those minimum standards.

Outside of the debate as to whether the standards are good and whether or not they protect inspectors, the SOPs are most often misused.

They get misused by inspectors who are stuck in the past, twenty five years ago or more, as an excuse for the fact that they (the inspectors) are becoming irrelevant.

Let me give you an example;

I know that checking for recalls isn't a part of the minimum standard. It's up to an inspector to decide if they want to check for recalls as part of their inspection and offer superior service to their clients. I personally believe that checking for recalls will eventually become a standard, and I think it's silly that we argue about how far an inspector's head should go into the corner of an attic and don't acknowledge as an industry that one in every ten homes he inspected in the last year had a known fire hazard right there in the kitchen staring him in the face. The solution was simple, it was available for free, and it's from a major sponsor of every association and inspector event everywhere, and it's *RecallChek*.

For now, it remains beyond the standard and I like that it's considered a "premium" service. It's giving inspectors an edge in their market and making them more successful.

In one major market out west, I have three incredibly competitive multi-inspector firms offering RecallChek with every inspection, and about 30 smaller (what we call "big companies in development") firms doing the same. I've visited there, done presentations to real estate offices, and in every resource area in those real estate offices I found colorful, well done fliers from inspectors who focused on USPs like RecallChek, 90-Day Warranties, and even our Termite Protection Plans. Now many of them have added SewerGard and MoldSafe as well.

I say all this because there is an inspector in this market whom I've known for many years, and while he was never a client I thought we were on very good terms. Until one day I was at an inspector conference, sponsoring the event, and he came up to me and asked how things are going.

I say, "Never been better!"

I was having a good show, probably 30% of the attendees had already signed up for *RecallChek*, which he had noticed, and it bugged the heck out of him.

You see, this inspector, we'll call him Manwich just to avoid using anyone's name, has been inspecting for decades. He's been in leadership positions in a major association, he's known the guys on the committees that come up with the standards for years and years...and Manwich is the kind of inspector who uses the SOPs in the wrong way.

When a client calls Manwich to get a price, and they ask if he uses an IR camera, if he checks for recalls, if he offers a warranty, or asks any other question about his services that go beyond the bare minimum required by the association's SOPs that he subscribes to, the answer is a very bitter, "No, that's not a part of our standards." He goes on to insult the other companies to the prospective client, which ultimately results in him not getting the order, and he's losing a *lot* of business to the competition.

His business is no longer about the customer, it's no longer about having fun doing what you do, it has become a losing battle.

Every time I see him at a convention, the clients who choose someone else after asking him a question he's uncomfortable with become more and more frequent.

Don't get me wrong, it's not just *RecallChek* or 90-Day Warranties and it's certainly not my personal influence exclusively causing these problems for him. The companies I deal with in his area are creative and competitive and they're coming up with new ways to get business all the time.

I'm just the most noticeable cause of his problems.

What I had been mistaking for an inviting humor-filled smirk all these years was actually a disdainful, "you jerk" kind of look. I had no idea! I think I handled his venting pretty well, but he refused to take any responsibility for his own failures. He actually suggested that he had the influence to change the SOP in such a way that inspectors would not be allowed to go beyond it.

I suggested why he was at it to go ahead and set the pricing for the industry as well. I was being sarcastic, but apparently that is also an issue for him.

Don't be a Manwich. The SOP is a minimum standard. What really matters is what clients want and what will make you appealing as a company to hire for a home inspection. I'm pretty sure you can pass high school with a D- and do only the required activities every day- I just never thought to try.

Stay *hungry* my friends.

Chapter 16
A Good Inspection is Only Part of the Business

Dan Huber of Inspection Support Network

The inspection industry has changed dramatically over the years, especially over the past five to ten years. As a result, the expectations of buyers, sellers, agents, insurance companies, property management companies and others have changed especially in regards to professionalism, differentiation, consistency, and convenience.

There are many ways in which you can achieve all four, most of which are very manual processes. Of course the automated solution for all of these things in the home inspection profession has been my life's work, Inspection Support Network (often referred to as ISN, serving thousands of inspection companies).

Now let's take a look at your target clients. They're oftentimes unfamiliar with the inspection process, they buy a home maybe once every seven years, and they are making the largest and most stressful purchase of their life.

As a professional property inspector you understand an inspection is complicated. You know the average inspector is looking at hundreds of things the buyer does not even consider or understand. You know an inspection is not simple, but the truth is, the buyer wants it to be.

The buyer is often worried about things such as, "will I qualify for the loan", "will the appraisal be okay", "did I pay too much", "will the kids like the new school", "will my old house close escrow", "can I afford this new house", "can I maintain it", "will I be able to furnish it".

By the time the agent or buyer wants to order an inspection the process has been tedious. Most likely there have been endless house hunting excursions, looking at open houses, new home tracts, older houses, etc. Many were either too big or small, too much work, too high priced... you get the idea. Then they finally put in an offer only to lose out to a higher bid or get put through a bunch of red tape by a bank or a difficult seller.

Finally, they get an offer accepted and they need an inspection within their contingency period. When the time finally comes, all the buyer (and agents) really want is to be able to easily order their inspection, and know they can rely on a thorough, professional inspector to help them through the process.

Can they call your inspection company and get a helpful, upbeat professional to answer their questions, and get an inspection appointment that will work for the buyer, agent, and seller? Can they go to your website or Facebook page and order an inspection if it is after hours or if they are more comfortable on the computer than the phone? Most surveys show the 40 year old and younger demographic prefers using the computer.

You must offer several different ways to allow clients to order inspections or your competition will and you will lose market share (yes, even in your area). In addition, today's buyers expect you to help them with all their inspection needs. You do not need to perform all of them if you do not want to, but you should be able to coordinate them. This creates a one stop bundling of services you can help them with while making money on all of them, even if some are outsourced. Besides providing whole house inspections, you may wish to consider mold inspections, termite, radon, 203K, pool, decks, stucco, phase inspections, commercial, thermography, roof, 4-point inspections, wind mitigation and anything else commonly necessary or utilized in real estate transactions in your area.

When you simplify the inspection process, and achieve the same level of professionalism and convenience that every other business they deal with on a regular basis does, you win- especially when your competition falls short.

The reality in home inspection is that the number of inspections that will take place in your market this week, this month, and this year is outside of your control. The portion of that business that you get is what matters, and the more impressive your offerings the better your take will be from that business.

So how do you get the maximum potential out of your market?

Let's start with differentiation. I won't spend very long on this topic since it is covered elsewhere in the book, but when I look at the companies in my system of thousands of inspectors, the ones at the top of revenue and volume tend to be inspectors that offer satisfaction guarantees, warranties, RecallChek reports, and other differentiators or extend their service into infrared, mold testing, and more.

Simply offering these as a part of your inspection will bring you some level of success, but if you want them to really have an effect on your business you have to market them well and at a very high frequency.

Assuming you can do that, all that is left is professionalism, convenience, and consistency, all three of which are my specialty as the leading administrator in the home inspection industry. Let me take you through the ultimate process for a home inspection to give your clients the convenience they are looking for, give agents that refer you the professionalism that will generate more referrals, and give you the consistency that will ensure business growth and liability reduction.

Step 1: The Order

Today the most competitive inspection companies in the market take orders in at least two ways: On the phone and on their website.

Phone orders are of course the most common, but there is a growing trend in the industry for web-based orders. When I say "web-based order", I'm not referring to a simple form that results in a phone call back to the client- I'm referring to an actual order confirmed, priced, and placed on the schedule, all done with a few clicks from a website. Your prospective clients, especially younger ones, expect this capability because they experience it in other areas of their life.

By simply having the tool there, as well as on your Facebook page for your company and as an app for mobile devices for your referring agents, you become the more accessible and professional inspection provider.

Step 2: The Confirmation

Within minutes of an inspection order, a confirmation email should be submitted. When the confirmation goes out to all parties- buyers, agents, third party providers of services, etc., the chance of a cancellation goes down substantially, especially when the confirmation email includes a mention of some of your points of differentiation and shows the professionalism your company can provide.

Within this process you should also consider integration, whereby the client data automatically gets imported with proper spelling and consistent details to your report writer and third party applications.

Step 3: The Agreement (and Payment)

With the confirmation should come the agreement, preferably in a trackable link, along with a payment option. Getting these two issues out of the way ahead of the inspection makes for a smoother transaction overall.

This eliminates the chance of forgetting the agreement on site, destroys any potential that a client could argue they signed an agreement under duress, and ensures the inspection can be released as soon as it is available- which not only benefits your client but also makes sense to your referring agents.

Step 4: The Inspection

Now we are in the part of the business at which most inspectors excel. Do a consistent and thorough inspection you know you will always be proud of. If clients attend the inspection, remember they are your paying clients. Do not talk over their head or be too technical. Think how you would want your accountant or attorney to talk to you when it is not your field of expertise. Walk them around the property to go over the summary items while being complementary about some of the good points you noticed.

Make sure the client understands how to read and utilize your report including when and how you will deliver it to them.

Step 5: The Inspection Delivery

Delivering your inspection report should be done utilizing a trackable link, automatically to any parties to whom the inspection report should be released. This is where an integrated system like ISN really shines, because not only does it achieve that delivery, it also brands exclusively your home inspection company as well as the agent (not a software provider).

Step 6: The Follow Up

After your inspection is complete and your report is delivered, make sure you send a follow-up email to your client offering to answer any questions they might have. This is a great relationship builder and it will show you were available even after the inspection, which might help reduce your liability if needed. Including a paid invoice with this follow up email is a great touch and may save you a few unwanted calls come tax time. Following up with your clients after the inspection via email is also a basic business process. Including the agents contact information and maybe their photo in the client follow up email is a great way to stay in touch and show agents you will help market them when possible, a feature you'll find at Inspection Support Network exclusively.

Now that we have the process down, at least in summary, let me make a few suggestions that will help you deliver the best product possible to each and every client while also impressing the agents you want referrals from.

1. Make sure you attach your Standards of Practice and or Code of Ethics via a link in the report.

2. Use a numbered summary with photos. Buyer's agents are put in the position of needing to write counter offers to the seller's agents after your inspection. This allows the Buyer's agent to have a simple counter offer written something like this:
"Buyers, (the Smiths) ask the Sellers (the Petersen's) to repair 1, 2, 5, 7, and 10 on the inspection report summary". Help make the business process easier and you will see your client and agent referrals grow monthly.

3. Make it easy for the agent and the client to understand your remarks. Remarks should be short and to the point.

For residential inspections I am not a fan of narrative remarks as they are usually too long and hard for your client to understand. Be thorough but make sure you are using language and descriptions they understand.

4. Make sure your report looks appealing to read. Do not forget the importance of a great looking product.

5. Make sure your clients have the ability to order an inspection via an attentive, knowledgeable professional on the phone; not an inspector between inspections or in a crawl space.

6. Have an easy to navigate, friendly, professional website.

7. Make sure (and advertise) that your company can provide or arrange for all potential inspection needs no matter the type or scope of inspection services requested.

8. Have a system that allows agents to quickly and easily access past inspection reports their clients were involved in.

9. Stand behind your product/service, and guard your reputation with your life. If a frustration from a client or agent can be turned into a marketing opportunity for a small amount of money or time, get your checkbook out.

As a real estate agent of 20+ years, I can tell you that agents want to know you are a fair, calm, respectable professional who will be a good communicator and report fairly on the facts relating to your inspection.

The Inspection Industry is a young industry. It is changing quickly and becoming more professional everyday.

Go out there and stake a claim of your market share. It is there for the taking!

Chapter 17
Work on Your Business. Not in it.

Paul Zak of America's Call Center

There's one simple thing you can do, more effective than any other, to help your business grow and succeed. It's about getting yourself out of the middle of everything, off the hamster wheel, so your business can grow faster. It's about avoiding the mistake 80% or more inspection companies make that holds them back from the success they really should be seeing.

Here's the key message: Work on your business and not in it.

Organize your inspection business so you don't have to personally do every single part of it yourself. Do this and you will leap ahead of at least 80% of all other inspection companies. Plus, you'll get to do the things you enjoy and have a less stressful life.

What does this really mean...work on your business and not in it? How can it be done? Let's take a look.

"Working on your business and not in it" is a key point from Michael Gerber's book "The E-Myth Revisited, Why Most Small Businesses Don't Work and What to do About It". It's a brilliant yet simple concept for all small businesses, but especially so for inspection businesses. Those who work in their business believe they personally have to do everything, they are the center of everything, and everything must be done by them. No help, no delegation, they have to do it all. Every phone call, every email, every part of their business must be done personally by them because (1) no one can do it as good as they can, or (2) they don't know there is good quality and affordable help available. It's the typical small business, entrepreneur dilemma...the owner who believes it all must be done by him, every action, rests on his shoulders.

Why did you start your inspection business anyway? You did so mainly because you love to inspect and you wanted the freedom, benefits, and rewards of running your own inspection company. You are the inspector. You are the company owner. It's your show and you are going to make it happen. Its' your baby.

But here's the problem with us small business owners...we tend to be control freaks. We believe we have to do everything. No one can do it as good as we can, right? Even when it comes to parts of our business we're not so good at or should not be doing ourselves that chew up a ton of our time.

Add up the time you spend trying to do it all. The phone calls, emails, typing and re-typing...the time you spend being a phone person, typist, and secretary take a lot of your time. Do you realize the hours and hours per year you spend being your own administrative assistant and phone person? It's eye opening when you add up the time each week, month, and year you spend doing these things, taking away time you could be spending building your business and spending with your family.

Look at a typical inspection, for example. The original call takes about 10 minutes plus or minus, follow up calls to get missing information, access, etc. take another 10 minutes. Typing the information into your management system or database takes another 10 minutes, re-typing the same information into your reporting software takes another 10 minutes. That's 40 minutes per inspection, at least (it is probably much more than that). This is time you are spending playing phone person, typist, and secretary.

Now multiply your inspection volume times 40 minutes per inspection. For example, if you are doing 300 inspections per year, that is 12,000 minutes or 200 hours. What could you do with an extra 200 hours per year? 200 hours is 25 working days...what could you do with an extra 25 working days to build your business?

And if you value your time at $125 - $150 per hour, as most inspectors do, you are spending at least $25,000 - $30,000 per year of your time being a phone person, typist, and secretary.

No matter what your inspection volume is, you are spending too much of your time being phone person and secretary. Just use this formula --- 40 minutes X [your inspection volume] = the number of minutes you spend being phone person and secretary. It is also likely for you it is more than 40 minutes per inspection, too.

Just the time you spend on the phone is way too much and not the best use of your time, preventing you from building your business and doing what you love. Calls about booking the inspection, follow up calls with the involved parties to confirm and finalize the inspection appointment, longer calls from "shoppers" shopping around for an inspector, the voicemail messages to return every day, the missed calls that could have been a booked inspection but "they already scheduled with someone else", the calls or voicemail messages about past inspections, some of which catch you unprepared. These are a sample of calls that weigh an inspector down when he believes he must answer his own phone.

The typical inspector spends far too much of his time working his phone like a phone person and secretary, adding to his stress and taking away time he could be using to build his business and do what he loves to do...inspect. Has there ever been an inspector who got into the inspection business because he really wanted to be a phone person and secretary?

The pleasant truth is there are people, services, and technology that can take all this off the inspector's shoulders, save him time, money, get him more inspections, get him more money per inspection, and present the best image of him/her as a professional inspection company. There are inspector-focused call centers and business management systems offered by companies serving inspectors exclusively, been around the inspection industry a long time, with a proven track record of saving inspectors time, money, getting them more inspections, more revenue per inspection, and ensuring their professional image to their clients and agents. These companies offer services that allow the inspector to work on his business and not in it, so he doesn't have to do everything himself, but instead the things he loves to do. The result is less stress, more time, more growth faster, and a more successful inspection company.

So take a look around the inspection industry for people, services, and technology that can take your inspection business to the next level. Look around in the inspector magazines, newsletters, conferences and seminars. Ask other inspectors. Hit the message boards, like www.homeinspectionforum.net. The major and meaningful companies to help you will easily pop to the surface. These companies offer services to help you be more successful, as they and you all share that same goal.

An area I am most familiar with is inspector call centers- we work with hundreds of successful inspectors at America's Call Center.

The first thing you need to do in your home inspection business to get an immediate bump in efficiency is have an idea of how much help you are looking for from a call center or an administrative employee. Do you need a person on staff, full-time, answering your calls? For some inspectors the answer is yes, for most the answer is no.

If you're in the latter category, look at a call center solution. The ROI is incredible.

If you are of the size that an administrative employee might be an option, take a look at the costs of such an endeavor before embarking on it. I've seen companies get too heavy on overhead too quick, and it is easy to do when you consider the cost of a full-time employee.

If you decide to look at the call center option, determine how much support you want to meet your needs. The general rule of thumb is the more support you want from a call center, the more important becomes their depth and breadth of services, skill level, experience, taking most or all of the "phone person" work off your shoulders, and giving you the most value.

Then call them. Yes, interview them. Be sure you ask about their inspection experience, how many inspection companies they serve and for how long, how they operate, their systems and who they are integrated with, how much phone work they can take off your shoulders, the kind of staff they have, how inspection knowledgeable they are, how much will they sound and act like your company, and do they mold to you or do they ask you to change your business for them.

Also ask around about them. Call fellow inspectors or ask when you see them at meetings or conference, or ask on the message boards. Ask other companies whose services or products you use for their opinion. The best companies serving inspectors know a bit about the other best companies serving inspectors, and this goes for any type of vendor.

Circling back to our main topic and to summarize, working in your business is doing everything yourself, even when it is a bad use of your time. Working on your business is taking yourself out of the middle of everything, doing the parts you enjoy and putting in place more cost-effective services and technology to do the parts not worth your time and the things you least enjoy doing.

In home inspection, the easiest task to hand off to another, whether it be an outside contractor or a new staff member, is the administrative side. Hiring another inspector is of course something you may be considering in the future, but that individual will require much more training from you. The reality is for most inspectors there is a huge amount of trepidation in sending an inspector out to perform inspections in their name.

It has been proven time and time again for many years that outsourcing the tasks associated with booking orders, confirming inspection, and handling administrative duties is a catalyst for growth.

Chapter 18
Making more money and Keeping it.

Bob Pearson of Allen Insurance

I've been around the inspection business long enough to be an expert in two areas. The first is which inspectors make more money than others. The second is how to keep it, which is my specialty of course.

The first thing the best money-makers in this business all have in common is that they always answer the phone.

I probably call more home inspectors on any given day than anyone in our industry. I estimate 75 to 90 percent of my calls go to an answering machine – it begs the question of how many inspections did you miss?

The second thing the best money-makers in this business have in common is a great website.

There are many great companies to help you with your website of course, but I would suggest first looking at ww.ultimateinspectorwebsites.com or talk to Dominic Maricic. Most importantly, make sure you have the ISN scheduler on your website, since many potential clients want to do everything on computers, tablets or phones.

The third thing the best money-makers in this business have in common is a great pricing model.

If you are at 80% or greater of your capacity **raise your prices** – if you're below your desired capacity and you are raising your prices it is not a business decision. It is an ego decision. The most successful inspectors in the business put business first.

The fourth thing the best money-makers in the home inspection business have in common is a vast array of value-added services and one stop shopping.

I want my clients to do a lot of business of course, it's a benefit to both of us, so I regularly include fliers in my renewals from vendors like The Inspector Services Group.

Beyond the Unique Selling Points, offering as many services as you can and being the one stop shop is immensely important.

Indoor air quality is a must.

Whether you like what I have to say about making money or not, whether you want to be in that top 20% of the industry, that's up to you and you will make that decision. Whether you are in that top 20%, or the bottom 80%, you are still making money and one thing every inspector has in common is they would like to keep it.

Here is how you keep that money, from one of the most experienced in the industry when it comes to risk management.

Taking pictures will save you a lot of headaches.

Inspectors love examples to go with this, so I will give you one. In the picture below you will note horizontal lines above and below the crawl space vents. This inspection was performed by a home inspector in North Carolina in 2003. It was alleged that the home had significant structural damage that was missed by the inspector. The picture was taken well over a year after the inspection as part of the claim.

After the inspection, for the next year and a half, there were several hundred small earthquakes. Unfortunately, we were not able to demonstrate that the condition was not present at the time of the inspection, due to the fact that there wasn't a single picture of this face of the home.

The inspector ended up paying his deductible and was subject to rate increases after this claim resulted in $55,000.00 to the claimant plus all the costs associated with the claim (attorneys, etc.).

That is an extreme example of course, but let's look at the other extreme. In the next photo we see wet flooring that a claimant described as "obviously visible" at the time of the inspection.

Mike Casey asked the inspector if he had any pictures from the inspection for this area, and he did.

The picture above demonstrated there was no visible staining at the time of the inspection and the claim evaporated.

From an insurer's perspective, the more pictures the better. At the very least a picture of every elevation of the home as well as each room is a necessity. It doesn't mean every picture goes into your report of course.

Earlier I mentioned offering Indoor Air Quality services to expand revenues – having the ability to do so can also lessen your Risk! We do not get mold claims when sampling is performed – we do when one is not.

What is needed is to offer the service and if they reject the service have them do so in writing. Under these circumstances, I'm unaware of a claim we've had to contend with on any large scale and mold claims tend to be large, as you are adding the remediation cost to any other necessary repairs.

Infrared is a great Risk Management Tool as well.

The two pictures below tell it all. The first is what is visible to the naked eye, the second is what the infrared camera picked up. Pulling out an infrared camera to confirm moisture issues or have a second look at high risk areas (problem areas for the roof, foundations, windows, mechanicals) can uncover water issues you would not have seen otherwise.

In this particular case I truly believe a great service was provided to the buyer when the inspector was able to show what was going on.

My best suggestion to any inspector is to pay special attention to moisture issues, offer mold testing, take pictures generously, and use advanced technology wherever feasible.

That way you can keep more of the money you worked so hard to make!

Chapter 19
Implementation is Key.

Mike Crow of
The Millionaire Inspector Community

Believe it or not I oftentimes struggle with implementation. The distractions are non-stop. On the plane someone wants to tell me their life story, the phone rings every five minutes, even as I have attempted to shut down everything else in my life to write this chapter I've received 30 emails. As a small business owner, you can likely sympathize.

Sometimes we even create our own distractions – I need to run to the store, the dry cleaners, talk to the gentlemen mowing the yard...etc. I am willing to bet that many of you were distracted even before you finished this paragraph.

I was once told that Distractions are the number one reason people fail. Part of the problem is that we allow ourselves to become overwhelmed with all that we need to, or want to, get done. This is another one that I struggle with and have had to learn to handle.

I share this with you because some of you think you are alone with these problems when you are not. In fact, well over 99% of you reading this understand exactly what I am talking about. The rest of you need to get a life. Life is not always easy or relaxed – especially if you are trying to accomplish something. I find the same applies to my office and those that I share it with. They are constantly challenged with what they are going to work on, and what work is coming their direction. Of course, then there is always the fact that when you have as many people as we do at the office that someone is always having a crisis.

So I want to share with you a few of the tricks that I use to get things done. Some of this may sound simple, but they work incredibly well.

Sometimes when I sit down to write, it is easy – other times I have to think and think about what I am going to write for days. I have had the title for this chapter written for over a week and yet just couldn't or didn't know exactly what to say – until I got rid of all distractions, and boiled all of these implementation tricks down into simple categories.

Time-Blocking.

This may actually be one of the most powerful. I have taught it many times in the form of a two week calendar. Here's how it works;

Mark on your calendar when we are going to do something and then make sure it gets done. This works especially well for something that you have to do over and over again. For instance, we have a young man at the office that every Wednesday morning works on marketing packages so that our marketing person will have them on Monday to deliver to real estate offices. Before we time-blocked this we were always behind and in many cases never really knew where we had left off and therefore needed to start from the beginning.

This powerful technique is also talked about in Gary Keller's Book "Shift" which we sent out to our top clients, and the rest of you should get a copy and read. Your life can't help but be affected after reading this chapter – one of the main reasons is how he talks about time-blocking for marketing. The problem with so many businesses is that they do marketing when everything else is done. Marketing it is the first thing you schedule in your business!

Beat the Clock.

I look at everything I do as a challenge. Therefore everything I do I am looking for a way to improve it. I want to find a better highway (or route) to get across town. I want to find a better way to do my reports. I want to...

..Read faster – there is so much to read, if you can't read fast you will never get done or through even the important stuff you want to read. I also, of course, use little tricks like reading in line while waiting (standing in line is a huge waste of time – so read) – or time-blocking to read important stuff.

..Write faster – or in my case type faster...Typing is so great because when I make a mistake or want to say it differently it is so much easier to correct it...(i.e. faster)

..Work faster – I hear inspectors all the time tell me they can only do one inspection a day...sometimes this may be justified (but rarely) – this is a great limiting factor to their revenue and quality of life. I was always looking for a better and faster way to get the inspection done – it is why my Dad and I worked so hard on the routine that we have and, of course, the reason our report we use is set up the way it is.

Speed and Accuracy is the mantra I live by under this topic – the person that can get it done quicker and the most accurate (quicker – believe it or not is more important – though you must in the long run have both) will bury his competition.

So the game I play with everything I do is "How good did I do last time?" and "Can I beat that this time?"

Now we have been talking about doing everything faster up to this point – however let's look at this like golf. You also can play "Beat my score." How many inspections did I do last month? – can I do better? I think you get the idea.

Stay Focused.

I learned this the hard way and maybe it is because I am a little (some days more than a little) ADD. There are times when you have to be 100% focused on what you are trying to achieve. I played Tuba in band when I was younger and every year there was a contest. We were all encouraged to participate – so I did. The 1st year I did great and got a 1 (the great thing about this contest is that you are only competing against yourself and not competing against everyone else to get a 1) Unfortunately, you only get one shot when playing your music...so if you mess up you can't say – "oh let me try that again" – well not and get a 1". The 2nd year I was as prepared as the first but for some reason my brain wandered, and I was thinking about something else besides my music and because it had to be memorized, I lost focus for just a moment and didn't play about 4 notes – instant downgrade in my score – now I get a 2.

When we are doing our jobs there are times we must focus completely as well. Multi-tasking is great and you need to learn to do it – however you also need to learn when to shut it off completely. You might even want to make a list of those times – especially if they have ever caused you a problem. Maybe it is when you are typing up the notes on a report...maybe when you are running credit cards...maybe when you are driving (though this is generally not the case – unless traffic or the weather is bad)...maybe it is when you are walking across the street. You get the idea.

There are simply times when you must be 100% or even 110% focused on what you are doing. Figure out when these are and make sure you protect that thought space.

Delegate.

My favorite word in the whole dictionary...One of the greatest problems that most people have in implementing is that they never set themselves up for success. They plan on doing it all and I mean it all...Well I have bad news for you, there are only 24 hours in the day and there is no way you are going to get everything done you need to get done in order to succeed. I am not sure where I learned this – it may even have been as far back as Tom Sawyer when he convinced others to help him paint the fence – it is amazing how something so smart can be made to look like a bad thing. If you ever truly want to be a success you must first understand what needs to be done and then allow others to be part of your success. Quit being so greedy that you want to be able to say I did it all by myself. I would much rather say me and a few of my closest friends changed the world. Yes, you can be the figurehead but you must allow others the opportunity to shine as well to really move ahead in life.

One day my wife – as she was washing dishes – saw me sitting at the table reading. She started a conversation with "You never do anything around the house…" I was shocked and somewhat hurt even. So I asked what do you mean – I help a lot. Well you never take out the trash, or mow the yard, or vacuum or wash dishes for instance. To which I said – that's not fair. I asked Jonathan to mow the yard this morning, I asked Alex to empty the trash and I asked Elizabeth to vacuum and you said you wanted to do the dishes. That's right – you delegate everything and end up doing nothing…to which I thought for a second and replied – "You say that like it is a bad thing." Oh and it gets worse because now that the kids are gone we pay someone to mow the yard, clean the pool, and now help keep the house clean. The big thing I want to try and get across here is that if you are trying to do everything you will never be able to do the things that give you your highest ROI (Return on Investment) such as marketing or building a better business.

My wife understands a little better now and I think she truly appreciates the fact that so many little things are handled by someone else because she used to try and do it all and she had little to no time to enjoy life.

This delegation extends to the workplace as well. Even with tasks as complex as writing and formatting articles, Matt does it just as good if not better than I. Brad does a great job at making sure we have articles that are useful to our clients as well.

It is why I introduced Nathan and The Inspector Services Group to all of my members at some point – they make your life easier because they do so many things for you. His people handle complaint calls when you are on the 90 day warranty, he helps you have better automated marketing with the RecallChek, he helps make sure your phones are answered when you are taking care of other important things – like your inspection.

Work when you are most productive.

I think Mexico has it right some days. My daughter went to Mexico for an extended period of time to learn Spanish. One of the things that we all hear about but may think is a myth is that they take a siesta during the day (an extended break) and after the siesta they go back at it. Well I have to admit I don't take a siesta (not every day at least) but I have found I am at my best in the mornings...this is one of the major reasons that I do Coaching Calls in the mornings. I have also found that most people (though not everyone) are more productive during the morning.

When are you most productive? When I was younger it was somewhere around 2:00 AM, and I will tell you I could move mountains during that hour. I am sure it had something to with fewer distractions – all the kids are in bed for starters. I don't care when your most productive time is, but figure it out and then plan what you need to work on during that time. This is like bringing Time-Blocking and Focus together at the same time, except even better, bringing it together when you are at your best, and even more importantly, if you do it right you will set it up so there are less distraction.

The 75% Rule.

I used to call this the 80% rule, especially as I was working on putting inspectors in the field. One of the things that I learned long ago was the value of experience. In Gary Keller's Book "Shift" he mentions again the power of taking action. One of the top reasons that people don't take action is because they think they aren't ready. You will never be 100% ready – it is literally impossible.

Experience is required to get past the 75% mark. You can prepare and prepare and prepare but until you set the ship in the water you will never really know if it will float, and even then, will it be able to handle the waves and everything else that it is going to have to endure to get to where you want it to go.

If you had waited until you were 100% prepared for doing an inspection you would have never done one. I know because I have trained dozens of inspectors and at best they were 80% ready when we turned them loose, and this was even with a lot of on the job training. There simply is nothing that can replace the experience that they gain when they are out there all on their own. Of course, with cell phones and now the internet, they have more resources than any of us old-timers had. I wish I could have looked up the AC unit by the model number on the internet when I was at a house. How about that unit that was in the house but didn't have an outside unit – can we say geothermal – yes I had some knowledge but it would be nice to have been able to look up the unit and give my client more information for this particular unit.

There is also no way you will have all the information you want and need to market your business until you actually get out and do some. I knew that presentations were important and I learned a lot from ToastMasters – but again there is nothing like real experience when it comes to speaking. Then, of course, I chuckle when I hear people say "I am not very good at it so I don't do it". None of us are very good at anything unless we start doing it and work on improving it over and over again. Even with over 10,000 inspections I was always working on improving not only the inspection process, but also the way that I wrote up the information from the inspection, and especially with changing technology and environments we are forced to adjust regularly – well that is if we want to improve and grow.

So when you are working on something and you are afraid to pull the trigger, get over it. I will teach you a couple of quick little tips that may help. As you are learning you can take a couple of different approaches that will help people not want to kill you as much. For starters if something is new – tell people – let them know that you are working out the kinks. Now you probably don't want to do this with the basic inspection. Imagine if a pilot comes across the intercom and says, "Well I know for many of you this is your first flight – don't worry it is mine too" - Not very comforting. On the other hand if the pilot comes across the intercom and says we have flown (to let's say Boston) a thousand times and we believe we can make your flight more enjoyable with an in-flight movie – but this is the first time to test it in the air – you will most likely be willing to be patient with them.

Inspectors could do the same thing with Sprinkler systems. We have been doing inspections for years and recently started testing sprinkler systems – there is no charge for the test and if we can't test it for some reason we will let you know – on the other hand, we probably will be able to give you some useful information about your system if everything goes the way we plan. I tell inspectors all the time if you are just adding this to your list of services then do them for free for a while as you learn...but do them. This makes you more competitive and gives you an edge against your competition.

If I had waited until I was 100% ready to get married – it would have never happened. If I had waited and I should say if Susan and I waited until we were 100% ready for kids, it would have never happened. If people waited to hire us until we were 100% ready we would never have gotten even our first job. So once you have a plan and have most of the pieces in place then get moving. You may not realize this – however, even when they opened Disneyland they weren't completely ready. In fact, they were out putting signs on the weeds because they hadn't gotten rid of them before the park opened. Since then they have adjusted more things than you can list and, by the way, continue to change and adapt to this new world. If you have to put some signs on the weeds then do it – but get started.

Start doing presentations. Start adding different types of inspections. Start calling people - telling them about what you can do to help them. Start sending useful emails. Start testing new ways to answer the phone.

Stackables.

Do things, especially large tasks, in small bite size pieces. For instance my car – when I was younger – was a disaster. It was full of trash and needed to be cleaned. I just could never seem to find the time to get it done – it would have taken a couple of hours. Then I had a thought – I continue to bring trash into my car and hardly ever remove it except when I take time to clean the car. What would happen if every time I went through McDonald's I threw away a little "extra" trash. Now my car was pretty bad – but within a couple of weeks I could see the floorboards again. This was a valuable lesson for me.

When we started doing computerized reports (in 1988) we had to buy a special program to create macro keys – many of you have this automatically now and some of the programs even come with a full preset list of macros (phrases to use on inspections). It would have taken me years to produce the list of macros that we now use – wait a second, it did take years. However, I didn't wait years to start using them. After getting computerized and understanding the value of a macro key I found a program and started creating them – one at a time. Then as I recognized phrases that we used regularly I added to them. Painful isn't it? Yet, it works. I call this stackables – you may have heard how every journey starts with the first step, well this is true - Even better though with stackables. Once you have one piece, it is done - in some cases forever. Once I created a macro I was able to use it on every job from then on – yes we adjusted some, however many of them were good for life.

The same thing happened as we wanted to give people an informational booklet. It started with a few pages – then it became a little bigger as we added information. Now it is a 3-hole notebook and I haven't had to add anything to it for years and yet it is given out on 1000's of inspections every year.

The big thing that I am trying to get across to you here is that if you do things right then you are building stackables as well - Building a better and stronger business every day.

Let me tell you what some of our most successful clients have done. John Villella has created a new inspection type for FSBOs - Damon O'Donnell has created a new program for Pre-Listing (Market) Inspections – Jeff Donaldson has created a complete package for 11th Month Warranty Inspections. By the way, all of these started with simple steps and then grew as they learned and tested new techniques and strategies.

This is how you build a million dollar company and how you make a company that others will not only envy – they will want to copy and when you are ready they will want to buy from you – for a lot of money. It's also how you build an incredibly profitable company at any size- whatever you are comfortable with.

Chapter 20
Certified?

Mike Doerr of
The Inspector Services Group

My team works with home inspectors every day- we serve over 4500 of them- and each goes through a training course we call a "one on one" prior to engaging our services typically. It takes around 20-30 minutes for most, and the first thing I usually get asked is "what's the most important thing to say in my marketing?".

While the answer varies by market, there's a few things that matter very little.

Saying your thorough, that you're an "educated" inspector, that you offer good service, that you're a member of ASHI/NAHI/CAHPI/InterNACHI/etc. ...none of it works. I get literally hundreds of calls monthly from inspectors that have listened to their peers, branded themselves poorly, and need a boost to their business.

One of the tricks a lot of inspectors like to use is to say they are "Certified". Nothing sounds better than "Certified", and nothing causes more debate in the inspection industry either.

In September of 2014, Nathan did something awesome for me (sarcasm). Here it is:

When I saw this hit his Facebook profile and the Home Inspection Forum, I knew it would be a long day. How did I know? Because for years now I've been hearing from home inspectors how their "Certification" is better than the other Certification.

Sometimes they'll point to the ASHI Certifications and criticize ASHI if they're a member of another organization. Oftentimes they'll point to InterNACHI's "Master" Inspector and say it is something you pay for and it's meaningless. Then you get into all the certifications from different companies for environmental testing and energy audits.

Are any of these certifications bad? No, not at all.

Do any of these certifications lead to success? No, not at all.

It has statistically been quite the opposite when we look at numbers. Many of the inspectors we work with that are constantly focused on adding the alphabet to the end of their name have shifted focus away from their business. The process of being "certified" in whatever the course/process/affiliation might be seems to have an inherent component of indoctrination into how superior you are to other inspectors. This leads to some level of entitlement and inspectors believing, erroneously, that as soon as they place a badge on their website/brochure/business card/shirt/vehicle that their phone will ring off the hook as clients flock to their company since they are now the "best". I'm not saying they're not the best, for all I know you are the best inspector and your certification is the most meaningful in the history of the business. Congratulations.

Here's the truth about certifications.

They mean way more to you than they do to anyone else. Most are an accomplishment you should be proud of, many have a great seal you can add to the bottom of your website or the back of your brochure. If you have a bunch of certifications and badges, it means credibility.

Most of the names of certifications in home inspection are meaningless to both the public as well as the real estate community. I'm not saying this to be critical, I'm saying this to prevent you from making a huge mistake by leading your marketing messages with a certification of any kind- that includes ours.

Certifications sometimes end up being a marketing nightmare. By creating a superiority complex, some inspectors become lazy in their marketing thinking that the certification is all that they need. Then, as is the case with every certification out there (except Certified Inspection Expert), the group offering the certification puts up a website where you can find all of your competition that has the same certification. You may as well forward your phones to your competition.

Here's the best way to handle Certifications, Unique Selling Propositions, and Association Memberships;

Always lead with YOU.

Your logo should be larger and more prominent than any USP, Certification, or Association Membership.

Keep your clients and prospective clients to yourself.

Don't ever link to an association, Certification, or other product from your website unless you are very confident doing so doesn't lead to other inspectors. We're very careful with this when it comes to Certified Inspection Expert, RecallChek, 90-Day Warranties, etc. Any of our links, banners, resources never link to your competition and you should demand the same from any provider of anything.

Lead with the stuff that makes the most difference to your audience.

If a prospective client is asking you about your services, maybe talking about certifications isn't the first thing to mention. Talk about your warranties and guarantees. Tell them what is in it for them. Then hit them with a certification they can understand. An example would be to say, "Each of our inspectors is a Certified Inspection Expert. We've been awarded over a dozen other Certifications and Memberships in the industry."

If the next inspector they call wants to wow the client with something specific, the assumption will be that you have that as well.

Get your input from a great source.

If you want to know what a certification means to your business, ask your clients. If you want to know how to be a successful inspector, talk to one that does twice as many inspections as you've ever dreamed of doing.

Probably 90% of the inspectors that call me have received some bad advice at one time or another, usually from local competitors or chatter on message boards. Vetting your source is essential- how many inspections do they do? What was their gross profit last year?

If you haven't been to a marketing conference, purely focused on business growth, I would highly recommend our Power User Conference or Mike Crow's 3 Days of Secrets Revealed in Dallas. Even if the content of either one isn't your cup of tea, the time you spend with successful inspectors is priceless.

Chapter 21

No Excuses

A Sample Chapter from the new book
Change|Up

Get the new book, Change|Up, at www.ChangeUpBook.com – until you do, we've added this chapter to the 2nd Edition of the Hungry Home Inspector, because home inspectors often ask us after they get done reading, "what should I do"? The answer is simple, do what works! Enjoy!

Right before I wrote this chapter I sent an email to 10,000 home inspectors, all of whom we either met at shows or already work with actively as users of RecallChek, 90-Day Warranties, SewerGard, MoldSafe, etc. It had a simple offer in it:

"I'll pay the first 400 inspectors who want it $105.00 to watch the 4 DVD set of our inaugural Power User Conference (2013)."

Of course the offer had terms and conditions, the first being you need to pay us $395.00, but in exchange you get $500.00 in lab fees from InspectorLab, so you come out ahead by $105.00 in services you'll probably use anyways plus you get the DVD set.

It may seem like a no-brainer to you and I. I set it up that way.

What should have happened is that I would lose $42,000.00 immediately in lab fees alone, another $4000.00 in postage, another $1600.00 in DVD printing, and of course the actual cost of producing the DVD with our staff of video production experts, but discounting that cost we are at a loss of $47,600.00.

We had a lot of debate around the office over how we offer the video of our conference. There were staff members who thought we should never release it, others that thought we should only offer it to those who actually attended, some who thought we should offer it to inspectors who attend the following year, and a few that thought we should offer it for $1000.00 to clients only.

After all, the value of the DVD alone is immense. If you wanted to see the event live, you would have to pay $300.00-$500.00 for the ticket, $400.00 for the hotel room, plus around $400.00 for the flight, all in all around $1300.00. Plus the event is exclusively for clients, so even being invited requires spending some amount of money.

We made the offer anyways, almost as an experiment. Here is an event where around 200 of the largest inspection companies in the world come for marketing advice- and you get all 10 hours of it to watch in your home at your convenience and we even pay you $105.00 to watch the thing.

The results were as follows:

1. We did not hit the 400 orders in the first day. It took over two weeks.

2. Over 15% of the orders cancelled once we asked for payment (and almost all of them were non-clients).

3. Over 80% of the orders were from clients.

4. Most of the attendees of the conference on the DVD purchased the DVD.

If you're keeping up with the math, the experiment had almost the exact results our staff had hoped for initially. Around 5% of the DVD's delivered were to non-clients. Most of the DVD's went to attendees of the event, and the rest went to current clients.

So basically I spent $47,600.00 delivering my own clients a DVD. I consider it money well spent. Just like it will cost money for me to get this book into the hands of my clients (and it is exclusively for our clients, I do not want to train non-clients to compete with you), the DVD did as well. I am okay with that because those clients that watch the DVD, read this book, go to the Power User Conference...they grow their businesses. Since our growth is dependent on the growth of our clients, these expenditures are investments, and they have been the best investments we have ever made.

There were a couple of inspectors who shifted their mindset as a result of the offer. Two inspectors that ordered the DVD immediately sent me an email to cancel and told me they did not offer mold testing and made a mistake.

I asked both why they did not, and both had similar responses indicating their clients didn't ask them for it.

My response to them was that nobody was ordering Cappuccinos from McDonald's until they opened McCafe, and now it is the reason McDonald's is hitting record numbers.

Neither ended up buying the DVD, but both are now offering mold testing. It just took the right catalyst, which in this case was the McCafe argument, to get them to stop making excuses.

You and I both make excuses for not doing something that would be good for our business, and both of us need to stop doing that! We make up all sorts of excuses, don't we? Some of the time we look at the numbers and cannot justify spending the money, other times we think we can do something better ourselves, whatever the excuse is it's nothing more than an excuse. There are companies doing millions and others doing billions in revenue that have already figured it out...why do we resist taking their lead?

In the case of these two inspectors, I had to virtually give them a pump and some Air-O-Cells to get them to offer a service that literally every inspection company doing seven figures in the history of home inspection offers. You might read that story and feel sorry for them.

I wonder if there is a CEO somewhere looking at my decisions in the same way.

Let me give you an example of a very difficult decision I had to make recently to put something in place that literally every company doing a billion in sales has...and yet I made excuse after excuse before finally giving in.

Last year I decided it was my last year at the helm of Residential Warranty Services and The Inspector Services Group. The value of me running the day to day operations paled in comparison to developing new products, acquiring other businesses, and doing high level marketing projects like a new web development platform we will launch in 2015 or writing this book. So I hired a headhunter at no small fee to find a Director of Operations, and subsequently hired a Director of Operations at no small expense. The most qualified I could find.

This is where my excuses, the things keeping me from achieving, start showing themselves.

The first thing the new Director does is establish that we need to do some construction in the office to reduce noise in our call centers.

There's a few thousand bucks gone, but no big deal. I do not even review the thing- I take my own advice from Chapter 3 and I get out of the way. So far so good.

Then he identifies inefficiencies in how we handle phone calls, and the potential for long term savings on phone service that currently runs us around $50,000.00 per year. (Yes, that is our current phone bill just for landlines as I write this book)

Perhaps foolishly, I am still in the loop when it comes to capital expenditures, so the tens of thousands of dollars we will be spending on new phone equipment and upgrades to wiring throughout our facilities in Indy, Fort Lauderdale, and two other locations in the U.S. lands on my desk for approval.

There goes a few tens of thousands, a little more heartburn, but the long-term savings making it an investment I can live with. Approved.

Then comes the real panic moment for me as a business owner.

My Director of Operations comes to me with something we need. More specifically, a person we need. "We need an HR director," he tells me.

That is not an easy pill to swallow.

It is one of those moments when you have to think about all those 9600 inspectors who received an email saying, "Here's a DVD of something the leading inspection companies in the country, people who make many times over what you do, for you to watch and benefit from, and I'm actually going to pay you to watch it," and you start seeing parallels between their terrible decision-making over a few hundred bucks and wonder if you are doing the exact same thing over a few thousand bucks a month.

Big companies not only have HR directors, they have entire departments. My neighbor of 10 years was the HR director for a major jet engine manufacturer, and I think back to the first conversation I ever had with him about his occupation. I remember thinking how ridiculous it was that a corporation would pay that guy obscene money not to recruit, not to do performance reviews, not to actually make the company any money directly. His job, as he described it, was basically to make sure every employee at his company had the best benefits, he made sure the company was held accountable in delivering those benefits, and that raises and vacations were implemented. He even made sure birthdays were remembered and anniversaries of employment were recognized with gold watches and plaques.

I did not get it. Now I do to some extent. It is all about talent retention and saving money on training and recruiting. Employees should be talking about their jobs when they go home and when they are out with friends. Everyone in town should want to work for your exciting company. It is what every Fortune 500 company has, which makes it indisputable that if you are at the point of needing an HR person and being able to afford one and you do not...you are a fool.

So I get out of the way, and just do what every other CEO does- take a perfectly round ice cube, put it in a glass, and pour the most expensive old scotch I can find in my bar over it slowly and try to forget the many hundreds of thousands of dollars that were just spent. Later I laugh about paying one guy thousands to find me another guy to pay a bunch of money to so that he can tell me to hire a HR director that I can pay a bunch of money to in order to make sure that we spend a bunch of money on our employees. Read that one twice and tell me you're not looking for a scotch yourself!

All of us have our threshold for what we are willing to make excuses for. If you are reading this book I hope you are beyond making excuses over a few hundred dollar one time purchase. Most inspectors in my top 1,000 list are at the low end not being quite sure about spending $3.00-$4.00 per inspection with ISN, in the middle not being totally comfortably with spending $500.00 a week on a marketing person, to at the high end getting nervous over $100,000.00 cash outlays for acquisitions or offering higher salaries for lead inspectors or business managers.

The more you can do without making excuses, the farther you will go, and the farther you go the less you will be making excuses. Did the chicken or the egg come first? I have no idea, but in this case dropping the excuses has to come first to some extent, at least to the limit of your ability to maintain the improvements you make for the short period of time it takes for them to have positive results.

Here is a plan you need to drop the excuses and just do, for two reasons:

1. *The cost can be contained and the results measured.*

2. *Literally all of the $1 million + home inspection operations in the U.S. and Canada have implemented the same things in all or in part.*

Just be glad you are not going to have to spend the money on an HR director anytime soon. These decisions are easy, and I have broken them down into 26 steps. Just like I do not need anyone to justify why an HR director is right for my business because literally every company that is creating the revenue levels I want to create has one, you do not need to justify anything here either because when you look at the home inspectors making the most money, they have implemented most or all of the list.

Pretend you hired me as the General Manager or Director of Operations at your home inspection company and I gave you this list of things and told you this is what we need to do to get to $1 million in sales. My resume included working in the home inspection industry literally all my life, growing up in a multi-inspector firm that does millions, and consulting/serving over 80% of the $1 million + companies throughout the U.S. and Canada.

That is my real resume. Now here is the list;

A. Ensure 10-20 real estate offices are delivered brochures each and every business day. If this requires the hiring of a marketing rep, so be it.

B. Get updated brochures (a minimum of 5,000) and materials from www.UltimateInspectorBrochures.com or another reputable source, professionally designed, with the following Unique Selling Propositions included;

    a. RecallChek

    b. SewerGard

    c. 90-Day Warranties

    d. Offerings including Mold Testing, Pool & Spa Inspections

    e. Money Back Guarantee

C. Get the Power User Conference DVD's from Inspector Services Group, and have key personnel (Marketing and Administrative Only) watch it.

D. Have the same key Personnel read The Hungry Home Inspector.

E. Join the local REALTOR board(s) as an affiliate member. Establish whatever relationship necessary to gain electronic lockbox access.

F. Hire/Outsource Call Center Operations for booking inspections with extended hours.

G. Implement Mold Testing immediately as a menu item.

H. Add a summary page to Inspection Reports and ensure the rest of the report is done by system.

I. Ensure same day delivery of reports.

J. Establish banking relationship (as described in Chapter 11 of the book Change|Up).

K. Establish a regular mailing campaign (like the one described in Chapter 10 of the book Change|Up).

L. Hire inspectors (or assistants) as soon as the level of 30 inspections per month is established.

M. Implement ISN (Inspection Support Network) immediately.

N. Implement the RecallChek App immediately (using the ISN integration).

O. Add videos for the Buyer's and Seller's confirmation emails (like the ones found at www.InspectorServicesGroup.com)

P. Get booth materials from www.UltimateInspectorMarketing.com and set up a booth at local and regional REALTOR events.

Q. Implement the BAM Dashboard for sales efforts at www.BAMdashboard.com .

R. Book ticket for business owner and marketing/office manager for the Power User Conference at www.PowerUserConference.com and get on a regular CE program for all inspectors (company provided).

S. Get quotes once annually for E & O Insurance from Allen Insurance, InspectorPro, and others to compare rates continuously. Get suggestions from ISG since they cover E & O Deductibles and work with insurers in their claims processes.

T. Automatically populate RecallTrak data for referring agents.

U. Schedule a minimum of 1 sales presentation monthly.

V. Establish company as a S-Corp.

W. Create multiple websites, focusing on different areas and specialties. Outsource the web development.

X. Log into www.HomeInspectionForum.net , register, establish a signature line with links to your web page, and post at least once a week.

Y. Call around to a minimum of 5 competitors per month and get pricing and offering data to ensure you stay ahead of the competition.

Z. Get branded shirts and have logos installed on vehicles.

That is the short list. If you get through all of them, you will absolutely be doing anything and everything that every one of the most successful inspection companies in the country does. When you add up the cost it is minimal. Maybe a few thousand dollars is all it takes to be the biggest and the best. You do it, you will be wildly successful, and not everyone will be your biggest fan. The next chapter is all about coping with the consequences of your success!

Before we go on, let's talk about the list for a moment. A-Z. That is 26 items. Not one of them is particularly offensive, I am not suggesting in any of them to do something ethically challenging, so why is it that there is a very high likelihood that we will not have 100% of the readers of this book doing 100% of the line items above?

Excuses.

How do we get rid of excuses?

The only objection I can possibly imagine to the list above being a real concern would be budget. Let's say the cash outlay is $1000.00 to get half the list done.

I will let you in on a little secret. We only printed 2,000 copies of this book and we have kept records of exactly who received it. If 2,000 inspectors make their way through half of the list above, the effect on their businesses will be enormous, and since you have read this far I will extend you the credit. At least a few of those items will be from The Inspector Services Group, and I am confident you can get through half of this list on $1000.00...I will finance that. For all 2,000 recipients of this book. No interest, other than the interest I have in your success. You just have to own a copy of the Change|Up book and be a professional home inspector to qualify.

What's the key to success in home inspection?

More than anything else, the drive to succeed. We'll see you at the Power User Conference.

Whether you are in the title, mortgage, or home inspection business; whether you are a single-man operation or have hundreds of sales reps, this system will help you grow your real estate referrals!

Track every marketing effort, automate your email marketing, log every phone call, and have your staff clock in on one easy to use web application that works well on both PC and Mac as well as mobile devices. More than 450 real estate vendors already utilize the Broker Agent Marketing Dashboard; and you can too with our free 90-Day Trial.

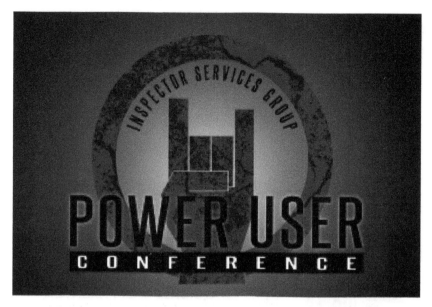

This is a Home Inspection Business Owner Conference

Pure marketing and business implementation. If you're looking to grow your business, you can't afford to miss this event.

800-544-8156
www.poweruserconference.com

Hungrier:
The 2nd Edition of The Hungry Home Inspector

By P. Nathan Thornberry
Dan Huber
Paul Zak
Bob Pearson
Mike Crow
Mike Doerr
The Inspector Services Group
All Rights Reserved
2015